DISCIPLES OBEY

HOW CHRISTIANS UNKNOWINGLY REBEL AGAINST JESUS

BY EDWARD N. GROSS

FOREWORD BY BILL HULL

Copyright © 2016 by Edward N. Gross

Disciples OBEY
How Christians unknowingly rebel against Jesus
by Edward N. Gross

Printed in the United States of America.

ISBN 9781498461290

All rights reserved solely by the author. The author guarantees all contents are original and do not infringe upon the legal rights of any other person or work. No part of this book may be reproduced in any form without the permission of the author. The views expressed in this book are not necessarily those of the publisher.

Scripture quotations taken from the New International Version (NIV). Copyright © 1973, 1978, 1984, 2011 by Biblica, Inc.™. Used by permission. All rights reserved.

www.xulonpress.com

Table of Contents

Foreword – Bill Hull ix

Preface xiii

Part One – Why Christians Rarely Obey Jesus 23

Chapter One – When We Start off on the Wrong Foot 25

Chapter Two – The Tale of Three Frogs 48

Chapter Three – When Love is <u>not</u> the most Important Thing 63

Part Two – How Jesus Obeyed. 93

Chapter Four – Christ's *Passionate* Obedience 95

Chapter Five– Christ's *Presence* Obedience 116

Chapter Six – Christ's *Perfect* Obedience 138

Part Three – How the Apostles Obeyed 159

Chapter Seven – The Apostles' Obedience-*Why it Matters* 161

Chapter Eight – The Apostles' Obedience-*With Flaws Exposed* 193

Chapter Nine – The Apostles' Obedience-*Whatever the Cost* 225

Appendices 271

Dedication

*I gratefully dedicate this book to my sweet wife, **Debby**, whose life has so often encouraged, helped and guided me in our exciting journey of love for our Lord Jesus and His Kingdom. The best is yet to come!*

Foreword

In the forward to one of my books Dallas Willard stated, "Obedience is the only sound objective of a Christian spirituality." That is a radical proposition, because it means that regardless of what theological school or pattern you have chosen, if it does not lead to following Jesus, it is useless. In fact worse than useless, it is misleading, even disastrous for millions of people who call themselves, "Christian."

Ed Gross also makes quite a claim, *"Disciples Obey."* I suppose some would like to fiddle with the statement, "do disciples obey because they are disciples or do people obey which makes them disciples?" This is the problem isn't it, trying to figure out what mysterious and complicated secret there is behind obedience, rather than choosing to live in the uncomplicated world of simple obedience.

The author becomes rude in a Jesus-kind-of-way in his subtitle, *"How Christians unknowingly rebel against Jesus."* What Dr. Gross confronts us with is the liability that pastors and teachers have in our leading of others. I think it is fair to say that the American gospel teaches that one can become a Christian, go to heaven and not follow Jesus. We have disconnected obedience from faith, producing a default gospel that is eating the life out of our churches.

I dare say that most people have been taught that faith equals agreement, that profession of faith is enough to make one a Christian. What it means to believe, to have faith, to choose Christ is encased best in the word "disciple." A disciple is a follower of Jesus. Discipleship takes place when a person chooses to follow Christ. That is when a person becomes a Christian. My thesis is that all who are called to salvation are called to discipleship, no exceptions, no excuses.

Dietrich Bonhoeffer stated, "Christianity without discipleship is always Christianity without Christ." Bonhoeffer defined discipleship during the Nazi period as the church's call to stand up to the Nazis and their persecution of the Jews and other minorities. He considered it a leadership issue. Ed Gross also calls leaders to stand up and take responsibility for teaching a non-discipleship gospel. That is what it means to "unknowingly rebel against Jesus Christ." Anyone who reads this book will no longer be rebelling in ignorance. Now you will be free to obey simply and freely whatever Christ has called you to do. I must be clear, you no longer have an excuse. It was Jesus who warned, "to whom much is given, much will be required."

Bill Hull

Author of *Conversion & Discipleship, You can't have one without the other;*

The Disciple Making Pastor and *The Disciple Making Church.*

Director of The Bonhoeffer Project at www.TheBonhoefferProject.com

Preface

This book is not short and sweet. It is narrowly focused and salty. And this is why. After what many view as His strongest statements on discipleship (Luke 14:25-33), Jesus asked an important question- **"Salt is good, but if it loses its saltiness, how can it be made salty again?"** The answer He gave to His own question is vitally important for Christians today. **"It is fit neither for the soil nor for the manure pile; it is thrown out. He that has ears to hear, let him hear"** (Luke 14:34-35). You and I can think we are helping the Kingdom and the world, when we are actually hurting them both. And sooner or later God will deal with us to correct that delusion. I pray that this book will help many sooner, before they are "thrown out," as Jesus warned.

That's what I mean by salty. Jesus often spoke about those who had ears to hear even what was hard. I hope you have a good pair of them. Because hearing ears lead to obedient actions. And obedience to Jesus may not be as optional a choice as you have been led to think.

When was the last time you heard that verse preached on? The one in Luke 14 where Jesus sums up His demands for discipleship with this jaw-dropper: **"In the same way, those of you who do not give up everything you have cannot be my disciples"** (v. 33)! It is then and there that He mentions salt that loses its saltiness (its essence) and asks us all, **"how can it be made salty again?"** The question begs this answer—It CANNOT be restored or salvaged. It is good for nothing. You see, giving up a little bit for the King and His Kingdom is not enough? He expects us to go all the way.

When He said this, Jesus wanted to get their attention. I am sure He did. I hope He got yours, too. In its context, He is telling us that how we deal with the issues surrounding discipleship will actually determine our usefulness to Him and His Kingdom! In fact, how you deal with discipleship will go a great way in determining your eternal destiny.

Thankfully, we are not salt! And so we are much more loved of God than salt is. We are humans made in His image. What is impossible with salt and with us is not impossible with God. He can re-salt us. He can renew us. He can re-track us on The Way (Jesus) leading down the path of joyful, immediate, loving obedience! And He is doing that all over the world today.

I want this book to help you walk down that path of true discipleship. To help get us started, please reflect on three words in my sub-title: How <u>Christians</u> <u>unknowingly</u> <u>rebel</u> against Jesus.

First—**Christians**. You will come to realize, if you do not already, that many Christians today do not follow Jesus. They have not heard His call and been born again and enabled to follow Him. That is why I prefer the well-used, New Testament term "disciples" over the rarely-used-in-the New Testament word, "Christian." I don't care if you call yourself a Christian. I want you to be a disciple who knows how to make disciples of love who will advance Jesus' Kingdom. Most of the first Christians did that. Relatively few today do. A look at our second word helps explain why.

The second word—**unknowingly**. I agree with the conclusion made by master-discipler Juan Carlos Ortiz. He, quoting Hebrews 5:12-6:3, stated that he thought the reason there were so few true disciples in his Argentinian Christian congregation was an issue of **training**, not an issue of sin. They were babies. Lapping up milk and incapable of reproduction. Immature. Only the mature can reproduce, he insisted.[1] Ortiz had been well-taught, like so many of us, but not well-trained. He had not been discipled and, so, did not know how to make disciples. That largely remains our Christian problem today. The good news is that repentance can quickly place Christians on the pathway of true, New Testament discipleship—with all of its amazing fruitfulness. But repentance TODAY, as in Jesus' day, must precede the great renewal.

Lastly, consider the verb **rebel**. When we rebel, we are rebels guilty of rebellion. We can rebel without knowing it. There are sins of ignorance. When our leaders do not call us to obedience to Jesus, we can easily become comfortable, church-going Christians. When leaders are not discipled, they no longer know how to make disciples. And, as I have shown elsewhere, the meaning and practice of true discipleship can be lost.² Indeed, it has been lost to many and that is why we desperately need a renewal of biblical discipleship.³

Paul summarized Jesus' Kingdom in these words, **"For the kingdom of God is not a matter of eating or drinking, but of righteousness, peace and joy in the Holy Spirit"** (Romans 14:17). Christ's Kingdom has rules to be obeyed. That is what Paul there was referring to by using the word, "righteousness." There is a righteousness that is imputed by God to believers—the very righteousness of Jesus. But Paul is not speaking of that in Romans 14:17. He is saying that the KING of the KINGDOM has laws that are to be embraced by us and extended to all (see 1 Cor 9:19; Gal. 6:2). When we reject Christ's laws, we are guilty of rebellion. Knowingly or unknowingly.

It is His Kingdom, not ours. We pray, **"Thine is the kingdom,"** not, "mine is the kingdom." The Holy Spirit empowers us to become **"slaves to obedience ... leading to righteousness"** (Rom. 6:16-18). Paul stated that from this beautiful way of life also flows peace and joy by the Spirit's power. Many of today's Christians want peace and joy without righteousness. Sorry, Paul mentioned righteousness first for a reason. With God, there is no "peace at any price." Peace fills the holy heart. And a life of holiness is one that is persistently obedient to the words of Jesus.

It hurts to see how many Christians today have a comfortable, distant relationship with Jesus on their own terms. They exist in what I call an **orbit** around Jesus. Whereas, in the New Testament, most believers were different. Reading those stories, we are inspired by disciples who have come into a discipleship relationship with their Lord-Rabbi Jesus on His terms. They were clear, demanding and life-changing terms. And one of the biggest differences is that true disciples then **obeyed**. But many Christians today only think about obeying. This book is a clear, salty call for us Christians to repent and follow Jesus as His true disciples into a future of tremendous fruitfulness, joy and suffering.

Though, it may not feel that way right now, I really do want you to be encouraged. So, I will speak the truth in love to you. I will often remind you of the glorious gospel of God's grace through Jesus. How discipleship is not at all about trying harder. But loving God and neighbor more **by the power of the Spirit**. And you will be encouraged by hearing how

Disciples OBEY

the simplest disciples TODAY, all over the world, are producing the most amazing fruit as they follow Jesus. I will also share current testimonies of disciples I know who are learning how to obey Jesus, even in places and ways many Christians do not want to. I have asked these friends to briefly write about the hardest obedience Jesus demanded of them and the results that came when they did obey. You will be blessed reading of their struggles and hopefully, will want to join them in following Jesus TODAY.

I will be concluding each chapter with a quote from the best Christian book on obedience that I have read – Andrew Murray's , "The School of Obedience." Published around 1898, it remains very useful today. Here's an example:

"Even when the vow of unreserved obedience has been taken, there may be two sorts of obedience—that of the law and that of the gospel…What the law demands from us, grace promises and performs for us…Grace points to what we cannot do, but offers to do it for us and in us. The law comes with a command on stone or in a book; grace comes

in a living gracious Person, who gives us His presence and power." (88-89)

So, I pray that as you read, God will bless and empower you all to fall in love with Jesus again, day after day, and prove that love by **"following the Lamb wherever He goes"** (Rev. 14:4).

Edward (Ed) Gross - December 2015

"The people were all so amazed that they asked each other, "What is this? A new teaching—and with authority! He (Jesus) even gives orders to impure spirits and they obey him." (Mark 1:27)

"They were terrified and asked each other, "Who is this? Even the wind and the waves obey him (Jesus)!" (Mark 4:41)

"All along the line we are trying to evade the obligation of single-minded, literal obedience. **How is such absurdity possible?** *What has happened that the word of Jesus can thus be degraded by this trifling, and thus left open to the mockery of the world? When orders are issued in other spheres of life there is no doubt whatever of their meaning. If a father sends his child to bed, the boy knows at once what he has to do. But suppose he has picked up a smattering of pseudo-theology. In that case he would argue more or less like this: 'Father tells me to go to bed, but he really means that I am tired, and he does not want me to be tired. I can overcome my tiredness just as well if I go out and play. Therefore though father tells me to go to bed, he really means: Go out and play.' If a child tried such arguments on his father or a citizen on his government, they would both meet with a kind of language they could not fail to understand—in short, they would be punished. Are we to treat the commandment of Jesus differently from other orders and exchange single-minded obedience for downright disobedience?* **How could that be possible?***"*

(Dietrich Bonhoeffer in The Cost of Discipleship, p 90)

Part One

Why Christians Rarely Obey Jesus

Chapter One

When We Start Off on the Wrong Foot

It is stunning just how dull we can be. How almost nothing truly amazes us anymore. That we can read the verses in Mark 1 and 4 and NOT be filled with awe is almost shameful. **Think about it.** When Jesus spoke to demons, they actually did what He said. And when He addressed catastrophic weather conditions, they changed. Immediately. This astonished everyone who experienced these incredible events. What's wrong with us?

Let's try to explore that question. To have been with Jesus must have been unlike being with anyone else. Ever. To have heard Him speak was different from hearing anyone else.

He affected everyone. Ruthless guards came back empty-handed and attested, **"No one ever spoke the way this man does"** (John 7:46). He was truly unique. And just before He left the earth, He declared, **"All authority in heaven and on earth has been given to me. Therefore, Go…."** Or put in other words, "I am God, in total control. So, GO make disciples and I will be with you!" They believed, went in the face of deadly opposition and found that what Jesus promised was true, **"the gates of hell cannot prevail against my church"** (Matthew 16:18). That was then.

This is now. We call ourselves and one another, "Christians." That is, we take His name—Jesus **Christ**—and identify ourselves as connected with Him. We go to church to worship. Yet, how easy it is for us, when His Words are read or preached, to yawn and glance at our watches! The thought of being in the actual presence of Jesus, the one true and living God speaking through His Word and issuing commands to be followed, rarely enters our minds. I repeat Bonhoeffer's exasperation: **"How is such absurdity possible?"**

Disciple - A Meaningless Word

Here is one possible cause for today's Christian apathy. Many who call themselves "Christians" are not true disciples of Jesus. Many of us don't use that word (disciples) in the same way He used it. We have read about "His disciples" repeatedly in the Gospels and Acts and have thought it was talking about people like us. Like most Christians today. But it isn't. George Barna's research concluded, "To pastors and church staff, discipleship is a tired word. To most laypeople, it is a meaningless word."[4] But in the first century it was a word expressing both great honor and sacrifice. Disciple had a clear meaning in Palestine back then.

Why is the definition of "disciple" important? If we do not know what the word "disciple" meant in the first century, how can we know if we are disciples? And how can we be sure that we have fulfilled Christ's last great command to **"go and make disciples of all nations"?** We simply can't. Do you realize that Jesus stated in that Great Commission that a disciple would **"obey everything I have commanded you."** So, to Jesus, obedience was key to both discipleship and fulfilling the Great Commission.

It is astounding, then, that Christians today who affirm both the validity and necessity of the Great Commission in their lives would be averse to obeying the commands of Jesus. But many are. They call themselves "Great Commission Christians." They give to missions. Yet they actually do not understand the Great Commission! That is how such absurdity has become possible. The demons, wind and waves obey Jesus, but many Christians don't!

Disciple - Much More than a Pupil

So, let's get on the same page regarding discipleship. What did Jesus and other first century rabbis mean when they called others to follow them as disciples? They did not mean come and be a student in a classroom. Merely listening and taking notes. Remaining at a safe distance from the teacher and hoping to receive a passing grade. As New Testament scholar Michael Wilkins wrote,

"From its very earliest use (in Greek literature), *matthetes* [a disciple] was not simply a learner or a pupil in an academic setting. In fact, Herodotus, in whose writings the noun occurs for the first time in ancient Greek, uses the term to indicate a person who made a significant, personal, life commitment."[5]

He applied this to the disciples of Jesus,

> "As a general principle, whether one was a student in an academic institution, or a follower of a militant rebel, or a devotee of a religious fanatic, the disciple was bound to adopt the lifestyle, teachings, and values of the master because of proximity and intimacy. Jesus recognized that principle: **'A disciple is not above his teacher, nor a slave above his master.'** (Mtt 10:24-25). Jesus' disciples would become like him."[6]

My research has led me to conclude that official disciples of first century mentors (later called rabbis) shared at least the five following characteristics:

1. Total Submission – disciples carefully obeyed their rabbi
2. Total Mastery – disciples memorized the teaching of their rabbi
3. Total Understanding – disciples grasped and accepted their rabbi's personal interpretations of the Old Testament
4. Total Imitation – disciples adopted the lifestyle of their rabbi
5. Total Duplication – disciples were committed to making other disciples

In *Are You a Christian or a Disciple?* I have shown at some length how a gospel-focused return to these five basics of New Testament discipleship is both challenging and transforming today's Christianity all over the globe. Even in the USA. Many other authors have been writing about this renewal, too.[7]

Why be an Oddball?

Wilkins is right, "Obedience to Jesus's teaching is the heart of discipleship training and it is the calling for all believers."[8] So, let's not cut "the heart" out of our discipleship! Biblical discipleship calls for obedience. But does today's church membership expect obedience? Do even our best, Bible-based sermons **demand** any obedience? What obedient responses result from our daily Bible reading? Or from our weekly small group studies? So, it is natural to think—why change my life after hearing a sermon or reading the Bible? Even those who respond to invitations for prayer and rededication soon get over it. It didn't stick very long for us when we did it. Why be an oddball and obey? Why take the risk when we do not have to? We are safe without needing to change.

Many of us Christians think we are going to heaven because we have "asked Jesus into our hearts." We responded to a gospel with few if any terms of our "relationship" with Jesus being spelled out. I pictured Him on the outside, so desperately wanting to get in that He would jump at the first stirring of my heart's emotions. But feelings can be funny things. Hot one moment and cold the next. Sensitive in a church service and insensitive away from that environment. Too often we have been allowed to decide what we want to gain from inviting Jesus "in." Such expectations were not the case with those who truly followed Jesus or any other rabbi in New Testament days.

New Testament believers were warned that, as His disciples, they would bear a cross[9], endure the loss of family[10], of jobs[11] and of dreams.[12] I believe we need to rethink the foundation, the starting point of our relationship with Jesus.[13] You see, many of us seem to have started off on the wrong foot. Are we responding to His terms or creating our own? His terms included: repent, believe, follow me, stop what you are doing, drop your nets, leave your father, don't miss the kingdom of God! Biblical discipleship is what a saving relationship with Jesus looked like. Today many Christians want "a relationship with Jesus" that rarely includes those things He required of His first followers.

Christians today are usually quite surprised to learn that the word "Christian" is not found in the Bible until midway through the book of Acts. There is no record that Jesus ever called His followers, Christians. It is used only three times in the whole New Testament! In our Bibles, the word "disciple" is what believers are called over 200 times!

The early believers knew each other as disciples of Jesus. In fact, the very first use of the word Christian grows out of the word disciple. **"The disciples were first called Christians at Antioch"** (Acts 11:36). They were disciples of Jesus before they were called Christians by others. Today we see exactly the opposite. We are first called Christians and then leaders hope that some disciples might arise out of the mass. But in the Bible, the only ones originally called Christians in Antioch were those who were functioning, committed disciples of Jesus. And disciples obeyed their rabbis. I am writing to remind us that obedience to Jesus was non-negotiable to His New Testament disciples. And it should be similar with us.

God is helping thousands rediscover and renew the reality and power of biblical discipleship in their own lives. I hope that this chapter and book will encourage you to join the growing global resurgence of true disciples who **truly live daily by faith in the presence of Jesus.**

I want you to take the time needed to reflect and respond after reading each chapter. Disciples obey. But not like programmed robots. They were always thinking, wrestling with Jesus' ideas. Asking Him when they were not sure. Arguing among themselves when they thought they understood more than they actually did. So now, to help you return to Jesus or to experience a true relationship with Him for the first time on His terms, carefully consider the end-of-chapter questions for reflection. And, just as prayerfully, consider the commands of Jesus concerning repentance as your first steps in following Him. Repent is a one-word command. It was the first word spoken to His disciples and it needs to be the first command we consider today! The only way to start off following Jesus on the right foot is by repentance.

Many Christians should Repent of their Repentance

Many of the Jewish leaders of Jesus' day were insulted by John the Baptist's and Jesus' call to repent. They were observing a long-standing way of life. Traditions that defined nearly everything that they did. Which they saw as going all the way back to Moses and Mount Sinai. Who were these men calling

them to turn the other way and live differently? For that is what "repent" means.

Similarly today many Christians are likely offended by the call to repent. We have been told that we are "in." And if we are in, we cannot be lost. No one can pluck us from His hand. That is true. But the question is, Are we 'in' or are we deluding ourselves, thinking we are safe when we really are not? Repentance is the proof that we are "in." John demanded it of the Pharisees and the Sadducees who were listening to him, **"You brood of vipers! Who warned you to flee from the coming wrath? Produce fruit in keeping with repentance"** (Matthew 3:8). Jesus preached repentance as His first word and taught His disciples to preach the same. Years later, Paul would describe his message to King Agrippa using the same words, **"First to those in Damascus, then to those in Jerusalem and in all Judea, and to the Gentiles also, I preached that they should repent and turn to God and prove their repentance by their deeds"** (Acts 26:20).

So, our response to Christ's Word should always be a sincere repentance or turning away from our sin and to Jesus. To a new and different life. We must deny ourselves and follow Jesus. Repentance sounds like confession of sin and looks like following Jesus. Make sure your repentance has both a sound and a look. I have never seen this truth better expressed than by the following quote:

> "The call to discipleship ... involves an about-turn and therefore a complete break and new beginning. To follow Jesus means to go beyond oneself...and therefore to turn one's back on oneself, to leave oneself behind...it can never be a question of a routine continuation or repetition of what has hitherto been our customary practice. It always involves the decision of a new day; the seizing of a new opportunity that was not present yesterday but is now given in and with the call by Jesus. Inevitably, people who are called by Jesus renounce and turn away from themselves as they were yesterday. To use the important New Testament expression, they deny themselves."[14]

When we repent of what the Spirit convicts us of, we begin to follow Jesus and really live. We start off on the right foot and get going in the right direction. Many Christians need to repent of their initial repentance, for it never included "a complete break and a new beginning." It only included slight changes that often relented and returned in the course of time. But not an actual about-face way of life that resulted from God shining the light on our prior way of life and convincing us that it was really the way of death. True repentance follows our grasping the reality that we were eating rubbish and calling it good food. True salvation occurs when the regenerating power of the Spirit shows us what our diet was and gives us a true revulsion for it. When He lets us taste of Jesus and makes us willing to change our life's menu. When Jesus becomes the bread of life to us and all the tasty tidbits of Satan begin to smell spoiled. Like so much rubbish.

What Makes our Good Works Good?

Following Jesus in true repentance, though, cannot stand alone. **"Repent <u>and</u> believe the good news"** (Mark 1:15) is the joint command Jesus issued in His evangelism. True repentance demands true faith. Faith in Jesus. Faith producing a relationship with One better than us all. This is really better news than we think. Many of us Christians understand this better when put in this way. We know that at the judgment seat of Christ, there will be some rewards given. For the saved to be rewarded by God, some of their works must have been truly good. Good enough for a holy God to call them good and give a reward for them. So, obviously, we can do good works. **"For we are God's workmanship, created in Christ Jesus to do good works, which God prepared in advance for us to do"** (Ephesians 2:10).

And we will be rewarded for those works when well done. **"God is not unjust; he will not forget your work or the love you have shown him as you have helped his people and continue to help them"** (Hebrews 6:10). Scripture sometimes calls the reward of good works "a crown." What makes a good work done on earth truly good before God? Something worthy of being crowned by God? It is when that work is combined with faith in Jesus. Or when it is **"created in Christ Jesus."** Paul elsewhere calls such works of obedience, **"the obedience that comes from faith"** (Romans 1:5).

Disciples OBEY

Do you believe that the righteous obedience of Jesus was so good that your faith in Him purifies your deed, making it "a good work" in the sight of God? His obedience really does do that, and that really matters. Because when you believe this, it will free you from thinking that obedience always leads to a self-righteous, holier-than-thou lifestyle. Looking to Jesus as you obey His commands will make you truly humble. This faith can make you really cherish Him every moment you live because you see the works you do as those you could only do **"in Christ Jesus."** They can't be done apart from Him and faith, alone, links us together.

As we will see later, Christians often do not even think about this amazing grace. We just go about doing what we think is right without really depending on Jesus. So, we are not actually doing the work **"in His name."** And many of us underestimate the command of God, **"And whatever you do, whether in word or deed, do it all in the name of the Lord Jesus, giving thanks to God the Father through Him"** (Colossians 3:17). Disciples act in Jesus' name, not on their own behalf. This way of life is not the normal Christian life as we have learned it. But it can become your new norm.

This is now how I live. One of the most important verses for my daily walk focuses on Jesus' promise: **"I am the light of the world. Whoever follows me will never walk in darkness, but will have the light of life"** (John 8:12). I believe this truth applies to me in every situation. When, by faith, I follow Jesus, everything changes. I see everything in a different light. We used to sing,

"I need Thee every hour,
Stay Thou nearby,
Temptations lose their power,
When Thou art nigh."[15]

Faith lets us live in Christ's very real presence. Hasn't your life proven that what Thomas a Kempis long ago wrote is true? "When Jesus is present, all is well, and nothing seems difficult; but, when Jesus is absent everything is hard?"[16] Let us all, Christians or non-Christians, repent, believe and live!

A 21ˢᵗ Century Disciple's Story

My name is Ed. I wrote this book, so you should know a bit about my life. I walked the aisle when I was 12. That same February night saw the conversion of my mom and younger brother. Jesus became alive for us and, by the end of the year, my dad was also saved. Mom and dad devoured the Word, obeying it as best they could. This led to tremendous changes in the family's lifestyle and direction.

Mom was our main discipler. But no one called her that in those days. She would study and obey the Scriptures during the day and share with the fruit of that with us at night. It was an amazing time of radical obedience and fearless evangelism. But, few of the people we reached were discipled. We simply followed the norm and took them to church with us.

Fast forward to today – four decades later. I have served as a pastor, church planter, missionary educator, seminary professor, author and radio presenter. All within Evangelical Christianity. But until five years ago I did not know the difference between a Christian and a disciple. That journey began when I was teaching Acts at an African Bible College. And it struck me—I was not fulfilling the Great Commission as the apostles did. Nor was I radically obeying Jesus any longer as I was trained to by my parents, or as the early disciples had obeyed Jesus.

My search into New Testament discipleship has revolutionized my life. The hardest obedience Jesus has required of me has been *true repentance*. The practice I called repentance involved confession of sin. But it did not demand rejecting the sin and turning my back on it to follow Jesus. Confession was all that was required. Struggling with the sin was expected. True discipleship has taught me differently. Sin is to be repented of, which involves both confession and an about-face action of heart and life. Repentance, though never perfect, looks like obeying Jesus in the power of the Spirit rather than falling back into an endless sin-confess-sin pattern. Since I was not seriously accountable to anyone, I could remain in ministry, managing my sinful habits, without living a life of holiness unto the Lord.

Obeying Jesus's call to "repent" daily has altered my life. I gladly guard my eyes and thoughts from lust, pray much more often, love others and give of my time and money much more radically than before my renewal. The Spirit guides me. I also live daily, looking for people of peace everywhere I go—just as Jesus taught His disciples to do. But I still do not repent or obey perfectly. So, I embrace the gospel of God's forgiveness every day as I confess and repent of my sins, looking to my perfect Savior, Jesus. In whom, alone, I am safe. And I have fellow disciples holding me accountable to a life of holiness as we all follow the living Christ. Come join us in really following Jesus.

Quote from Andrew Murray

"The only way to learn to do a thing is to do it. The only way to learn obedience from Christ is to give up our own will and make the doing of His will the desire and delight of our heart." (42)

Questions for Reflection

1. What exactly has caught you by surprise in this chapter?

2. How many Christians that you know match the five point description of a New Testament disciple? Discuss the results of our churches being full of Christians rather than disciples.

3. Have you been defining "repentance" correctly or confusing it with "confession?"

4. What do you think you should do as your first step of repentance?

5. PRAY right now for yourself and for others you know who need to re-visit repentance.

6. Discuss what makes our good works good.

One-word Command for Obedience

"Repent"

"The time has come," he said. "The kingdom of God has come near. **Repent and believe the good news! (Mark 1:15)**

They went out and preached that people should **repent.** (Mark 6:12)

I tell you, no! But unless you **repent**, you too will all perish. (Luke 13:3)

…and **repentance** for forgiveness of sins will be preached in his [Christ's] name to all nations, beginning at Jerusalem. (Luke 24:47)

Consider how far you have fallen! **Repent** and do the things you did at first. If you do not repent, I will come to you and remove your lampstand from its place. (Rev. 2:5)

Repent therefore! Otherwise, I will soon come to you and will fight against them with the sword of my mouth. (Rev. 2:26)

So I will cast her on a bed of suffering, and I will make those who commit adultery with her suffer intensely, unless they **repent** of their ways. (Rev. 2:22)

Remember, therefore, what you have received and heard; hold it fast, and **repent.** But if you do not wake up, I will come like a thief, and you will not know at what time I will come to you. (Rev. 3:3)

"Therefore everyone who hears these words of mine and <u>puts them into practice</u> is like a wise man who built his house on the rock… But everyone who hears these words of mine and <u>does not put them into practice</u> is like a foolish man who built his house on the sand." (Matthew 7:24-26)

"I have set you an example that you should do as I have done for you. I tell you the truth, no servant is greater than his master, nor is a messenger greater than the one who sent him. Now that you know these things, you will be blessed <u>if you do them</u>." (John 13:15-17)

"To commit ourselves to Christ as fully devoted followers, we must be struck not just with the benefits of our encounters with Him but also with the divine authority of the Person we are following and the cause to which he leads us. As we have noted, following is simply a matter of unqualified obedience to the incarnate God of the universe. If benefits alone were the motivation, the followers of the first century would have bailed out immediately, since for many of them" to follow" meant being marginalized, maligned and sometimes martyred."

(Joseph Stowell – Following Christ - pp67-66)

"Jesus had the pattern for forming disciples. He gave His own disciples concrete things to do instead of things to store away in their brains. And they obeyed Him. He didn't preach inspirational messages to motivate them…If we were under the lordship of Christ, He could just say the word, and we wouldn't need any soft organ music or soothing words from the pulpit—we would do as we were told."

(Juan Carlos Ortiz, Disciple, pp 110-111)

Chapter Two

The Tale of Three Frogs

Another reason why many Christians rarely obey Jesus is simply captured by this short but profound tale:

There were three frogs sitting on a log. One frog decided to jump into the pond. How many frogs were left on the log?

If your mind works like mine, you quickly thought, "two." We may easily conclude that there were two frogs left on the log because one decided to jump into the water; but our rapid deduction reveals a BIG flaw. You see, there were still three frogs left on that log. The frog who decided to jump into the water had made a great decision. He was getting hot and he needed to cool off. He needed to get wet. So he decided to jump in. But mental conclusions are not the same as movement. *Deciding* to do something is NOT THE SAME AS DOING IT!

When you are hungry and decide it is time to eat, you know that decision to eat is NOT the same as eating. It is only thinking about eating. There is no chewing or swallowing; no caloric intake. You cannot satisfy your hunger until you do something about it. Until you eat. Likewise, when you read this book, you might get all excited about what you're thinking. You might even start planning. But until you jump off the log, you are practically no different from those other frogs, which live and die quite comfortably right where they are.

When Doing Nothing Turns Deadly

In fact, you who read this might be in greater danger than those who do not. How can that be? This is how—if what you are thinking about doing is something that you ought to do. Something that God commands you to do; something that your family, your neighbors, your nation and your world need you to do. Then, staying on the log might be downright deadly.

"Anyone who knows the good he ought to do and doesn't do it, sins" (James 4:17). We all understand that sin is bad, but we have usually categorized "sin" as bad stuff we have done that we should not have done. Or the really bad stuff that others do. When James wrote that NOT doing what we ought to do is sinful, he was showing us how deadly staying on the log can be. **"The wages of sin is death"** (Rom. 6:23a). If all sin is deadly, then both sins of *commission* and sins of *omission* are destructive. What we do that is wrong and what we don't do that we should do, both lead to death: dying lives, dying families and dying churches. So, when a frog stays too long on a log, he begins to cook, no matter how often he contemplates jumping into the water. Is it possible that there are many well-dressed, neatly-groomed, church-going Christians who are drying up because they never get beyond the carefully-thinking-it-over stage?

Listen to Jesus. **"He who is not with me is against me, and he who does not gather with me scatters"** (Matt. 12:30). That is disciple talk. To be with Jesus is to follow Jesus. To acknowledge His presence. To walk with God. But you cannot truly walk with God without doing the other thing Jesus mentioned in this verse. When we walk with Jesus, we "gather." We stretch out our hands and pick up someone or something else. We do good for others out of love. What have you gathered with Jesus? Please think hard about that. The question is crucial because Jesus taught that doing nothing is scattering. Doing nothing is detrimental to the Kingdom and yourself.

Good, Church-Going Christians

So, we will slightly alter the original story as follows:

There were three Christians sitting on a pew listening to a good sermon. One Christian decided to change his life and follow Jesus. How many Christians were left sitting on the pew?

In writing this book, I hope to help you see the deadly condition that exists in much of Christianity. Maybe even in your church. A church culture that listens, reflects, and says, "Amen;" but returns the next Sunday just to do the same thing again. Riding a merry-go-round is not following Jesus. That type of Christianity is of little value to anyone. Such a Christian is not really helping others or pleasing God. Such a Christian is not a disciple or a follower of Jesus. He is just one of many churchgoing Christians. One of millions who think a lot about the Bible, about Jesus, about heaven and hell. But thinking is not doing. And if you are not following Jesus, obeying His commands out of a heart of faith and love, He does not see you as **"with me."**

I will not be giving false hopes in this book. But will follow Paul, who, when writing to a very faithful church, worded his warnings very carefully,

"Therefore, my friends, as you have always obeyed—not only in my presence, but now much more in my absence—continue to work out your salvation with fear and trembling, for it is God who works in you to will

and to act according to his good purpose" (Philippians 2:12-13).

We are in agreement with James that **"Faith without works is dead"** (James 2:26b). A past decision without ongoing obedience is a fruitless decision. A mere decision looks like **"the seed that fell among rocky places"** producing **"the man who hears the word and at once receives it with joy. But since he has no root, he lasts only a short time. When trouble or persecution comes because of the word, he quickly falls away"** (Matthew 13:20-21). Such a "faith" does not save that person. It is not true faith. Many of us have been assured that if we simply ask Jesus to "come in," then He will. And all will be well. We should have interpreted the gospel more carefully than that. Listen to what Jesus said, **"If anyone loves me, he will obey my teaching, My Father will love him, and we will come to him and make our home with him. He who does not love me will not obey my teaching"** (John 14:21-22). Wanting to be saved from hell is not the only or best motive for asking Him to enter our lives. He indwells those who love and obey Him. His terms of entrance are not quite as simple as many Christians suppose.

Conversion without Transformation

Of course, I know that it is only faith that unites us with Jesus. That is the wonderful gospel of God's grace. But we have created a mess by assuring people of a quickly achieved heavenly salvation without any earthly transformation. True faith must not be divorced from what it produces: works of love. As Bonhoeffer again wrote,

> "From the point of view of justification it is necessary to separate them (faith & obedience), but we must never lose sight of their essential unity. For faith is only real when there is obedience, never without it...."[17]

True grace, though abundantly rich and offered freely, is not easy. It is not a beautifully wrapped, batteries included, no-assembly-required birthday gift. THAT is most definitely not the gift of God's salvation by grace offered to us through faith. Jesus said, **"Enter by the narrow gate. For the gate**

is wide and the way is easy that leads to destruction, and those who enter by it are many. For the gate is narrow and the way is hard that leads to life, and those who find it are few." (Matthew 7:13-14 – ESV).

Bonhoeffer, who opposed and was executed by the Nazis 70 years ago, wrote, "Cheap grace is the deadly enemy of our Church. We are fighting today for costly grace." And, "Cheap grace is grace without discipleship, grace without the cross, without Jesus Christ, living and incarnate.[18]

I do not want anyone to misunderstand me. I carefully insist that our obedience, though sincere and real, is never perfect or faultless. It has no saving merit on its own. Our obedience always must be what Paul called, **"the obedience that comes from faith,"** (Romans 1:5), or a looking-to-Jesus obedience. We stand justified in Him. His perfection has become ours. We receive His righteousness when we first truly believe, with its fruit being imputed to our account before God. That is a great truth. It is part of the gospel which can help free us from both self-righteousness and self-condemnation!

I will often declare the whole gospel in this book to help counter the deadly sin of pride from growing in our hearts. I realize that we are so prone to exalt ourselves, that any long look at obedience runs the risk of focusing attention on us and our outcomes rather than on Jesus. So, this is the antidote—do not focus on obedience. Focus on Jesus. Listen to Jesus. And follow Jesus. Don't just sit on the log or in the pew, pondering Christ's commands. Be a disciple and jump in. But keep your eyes on Jesus by an active, humble, obedient faith. For a look at some of Jesus' commands and how we should obey them, see Appendix One: The Commands of Jesus in Mark's Gospel.

A 21st Century Disciple's Story

My name is Debby. I am Ed's wife. I grew up in a Christian home, and I was acquainted with the term "disciple." To me, a disciple was simply one who followed Jesus. I have come to understand better what a disciple really means and thus, how to follow Jesus on His terms. To be a disciple is to be totally submitted to Jesus, to imitate his life, to learn His teachings, to hide the Word in my heart and to become a disciple maker.

The hardest obedience Jesus has required of me has been *to let go of many things I cannot control and remember that Jesus, Himself is my main focus*. Embracing this has changed and yet simplified my life. Life happens. But I have learned too that nothing should come between me and Jesus. That simplifies everything. My family, job, possessions or goals are submitted to Jesus. They are gifts from God, but they must not get between me and Jesus.

In this journey of discipleship, I began to pray with others for "People of Peace" in our area. After some time, others joined us and God started opening doors. We saw God prepare people in our region, and even around the world, to hear and obey the call to "go and make disciples."

Along with committing to regular prayer, I learned the "Discovery Bible Study" method. Being a believer, I was accustomed to Bible Studies that were taught by a leader. I taught many such classes. These did not often lead to growth or change in my life. It was not uncommon for me to do little or nothing with the Word from these studies.

In Discovery Bible Studies I learned to respond to the Scripture with a concrete "I Will" statement that the Holy Spirit led me to make.

I will, with the Lord's help, do something in response to the Word and as well as share the story with someone else in the coming week. This simple change in format has ignited my heart in following Jesus. The outcome is regular repentance, growing faith, and open doors to sharing and making disciples.

Along with this, I have a new spirit of expectation. This approach to following Jesus has shown me the reality of the Holy Spirit being the Teacher and Jesus' going before me as He has promised in the Great Commission. Practicing the presence of God has become a reality and following Jesus has become both simple and duplicable. Come and follow Jesus with us.

Quote from Andrew Murray

"From the very beginning of the Christian life, let us avoid the fatal mistake of calling Christ, "Master" but not doing what He says." (58)

Questions for Reflection

1. Is your Christian environment characterized more by thought than by action? How much thought do you think should precede obedience?
2. Have you considered sins of omission as being equally deadly to sins of commission?
3. Can you clearly explain why grace is costly and not cheap?
4. Discuss how you could encourage more of a response to the Word in your home and church.

One-word Command to Obey

"Believe"

"The time has come," he said. "The kingdom of God is near. Repent and **believe** the good news. (Mark 1:15)

Overhearing what they said, Jesus told him, Don't be afraid, just **believe.** (Mark 5:36)

Whoever **believes** and is baptized will be saved, but whoever does not **believe** will be condemned. (Mark 16:16)

For God so loved the world that he have his one and only Son, that whoever **believes** in him shall not perish, but have eternal life. (John 3:16)

Then they asked him, What must we do to the works God requires? Jesus answered, The work of God is this: to **believe** in the one he has sent. (John 6:28-29)

Then Jesus declared, I am the bread of life, Whoever comes to me will never go hungry, and whoever **believes** in me will never be thirsty. (John 6:35)

I told you that you would die in your sins, if you do not **believe** that I am he, you will indeed die in your sins." (John 8:24)

Believe me when I say that I am in the Father and the Father is in me, or at least **believe** on the evidence of the works themselves. (John 14:11)

Then he said to Thomas, Put your finger here, see my hands. Reach out your hand and put it into my side. Stop doubting and **believe.** (John 20:27)

"One of the teachers of the law came and…asked him, 'Of all the commandments, which is the most important?' 'The most important one,' answered Jesus, 'is this: …Love the Lord your God will all your heart and with all your soul and will all your mind and with all your strength.' The second is this: 'Love your neighbor as yourself.' There is no commandment greater than these." (Mark 12:28-31)

"Let no debt remain outstanding, except the continuing debt to love one another, for whoever loves others has fulfilled the law. The commandments…are summed up in this one command: "Love your neighbor as yourself." Love does no harm to a neighbor. Therefore love is the fulfillment of the law." (Romans 13:8-10)

"So anyone who thinks he has understood the divine scriptures or any part of them, but cannot by his understanding build up this double love of God and neighbor, has not yet succeeded in understanding them."

(Augustine of Hippo – On Christian Teaching, 1:36.40)

"I have written almost fifty books, and everything in every one of them might be mistaken, but this one thing has to be true: that God is love."

(Peter Kreeft – The God Who Loves You, p 12)

"The apostle does not say, 'God is loving,' as if he were speaking of one of many divine attributes, but "God is love' —as if to say that love pervades and influences all His attributes."

(John MacArthur – The Love of God, p 29)

Chapter Three

When Love is <u>not</u> the most Important Thing

I magine, standing alone before Jesus. He looks at you and says, "I have a clear, one-word command for you. The one thing that matters most to Me and will prove that you are My disciple." Would you do it? You probably are thinking, "Sure, I would. No one matters more to me than Jesus."

<u>Love</u> is such a command. Does that thought surprise or confuse you? Do you think of love that way? Many Christians do not, because love is a state of being. It is, to begin with, an inner emotion. We forget **"God looks on the heart,"** and think that what we do outwardly matters most. You see, your heart's feelings matter to God. You love what you take delight in. Those people of whom you think often and long to see, you love. God has commanded us to love Him and others that way. Not occasionally. All of the time. **"Love the Lord your God with all your heart and with all your soul and with all your mind and with all your strength" (Mark 12:30).** As I wrote elsewhere,

> "Think of it! God was asked what mattered most to him. And he gave a clear answer. End of debate. No further questions needed. Never ever forget that, according to Jesus, love matters most to God. Does love matter most to you?
> "Don't answer that question too quickly or lightly. Really reflect on it.... Here's another question. Since love is the most important single thing, why should you ever allow it to take a second place? Why should love EVER be displaced by any other thought, emotion or choice in our lives?" [19]

Today's lack of love among Christians is proof that many of us are in rebellion. Do you think that is too strong a word? Isn't it rebellion when children defy their parents? Or when a citizen opposes the laws of the land? Wherever in the Kingdom love is not being exercised, the spirit of rebellion is. Christ-like love is hard enough to find in a church among its members. How difficult is it to see between Christians of different churches? Or varying denominations? Or with pastors in their relationships with other pastors?

One reason that some of us may not highlight God's command to love is that we often downplay God's commands in favor of His grace. As if they were opposed to each other. We have such security in our already being saved that obeying Jesus really does not play a big part in how we actually live. What you **must** realize, if you really want to be a disciple of Jesus, is that Christ's commands cannot be discarded. And especially His command to love, since it is not merely one of many important commands. It is the most important command for His followers. Love rightly defined can hardly be overemphasized.[20] Theologian Gary Badcock rightly stated,

"And so it is that with love, we are at the center of everything in the teaching of Jesus... When taken together with such Johannine statements as 'God is love' and 'God so loved the world' such texts (as Mk 12:28-31) rightly lead us to conclude that we have in the concept of love a kind of symbol of the whole of the Christian message, both in itsfoundations in the being and acts of God and in its application in the spiritual life. Theologically, everything is to be located and found here; everything is to be organically developed in relation to this one concrete concept."[21]

If our lives are not devoted to love, how can we claim to be following Jesus, who is Love Incarnate?[22]

The "House" of Love

Jesus was often called "**rabbi**,"[23] even by Nicodemus, a Jewish member of the ruling Sanhedrin (John 3:2). The term was one of great respect and honor given to eminent sages or masters who had followers. We have seen five ways in which Jesus discipled like other respected rabbis trained their disciples. But in reference to "love to God and neighbor," He differed significantly from them. And every rabbi who had some significant disagreement with the interpretations of others would need to establish his own "school" or "house."

Some understanding of Jewish history is helpful here. The most famous schools of the early 1st century were Beit Hillel and Beit Shammai. Hillel (died ca 10AD), the President of the Sanhedrin, was known to be more tolerant. Shammai (died ca 30AD), who succeeded Hillel as President, was more restrictive and politically reactionary. The school (disciples) of Shammai would have encouraged the Jewish rebellion that ultimately led to the massacre of thousands and the destruction of the Temple (67-70AD). Hillel's school, led by his grandson Gamaliel II, became the main leaders only after the devastation of 70AD. Though Hillel and Shammai themselves differed on only a few key matters, their followers in the time of Jesus and His apostles became divided in hundreds of ways.

> "The Hillelites were, like the founder of their school, quiet, peace-loving men, accommodating themselves to circumstances and times, and being

determined only upon fostering the Law and bringing man nearer to his God an the Shammaites, on the other hand, stern and unbending like the originator of their school, emulated and even exceeded his severity. To them it seemed impossible to be sufficiently stringent in religious prohibitions. "The disciples of Hillel, 'the pious and gentle follower of Ezra' (Sanh. 11a), evinced in all their public dealings the peacefulness, gentleness, and conciliatory spirit which had distinguished their great master; and by the same characteristic qualities they were guided during the political storms which convulsed their country. The Shammaites, on the contrary, were intensely patriotic, and would not bow to foreign rule.... Dispositions so ... antagonistic cannot usually endure side by side without provoking serious misunderstandings and feuds; and it was owing solely to the Hillelites' forbearance that the parties did not come to blows, and that even friendly relations continued between them, for a time at least."[24]

Enough Jewish history for now. Let's get back to the importance of "love" as the fulfillment of the law. All Jewish sages in the first century would have spoken of the importance of love. Even Shammai taught, "Greet everyone with a smile on your face."[25] Those Jews knew the Torah well. Its holy commands declared that it was never right to lay love aside.

In our day, many Christians have wondered about the relevance of the disturbing and severe "Imprecatory Psalms" in our lives. Interacting with one of those psalms in which the author begins to rail against his oppressors and the haters of God, Eugene Peterson made this helpful comment:

> "We can't excuse the psalmist for getting angry on the grounds that he was not yet a Christian, for he had Leviticus to read: 'You shall not hate your brother in your heart.... You shall not take vengeance or bear a grudge against the sons of your ownpeople, but you shall love your neighbor as yourself' (Lev 19:17-18 RSV). And he had Exodus: 'If you meet your enemy's ox or his ass

going astray, you shall bring it back to him. If you see the ass of one who hates you lying under its burden, you shall refrainfrom leaving him with it; you shall help him to lift it up" (Ex 23:4-5). And he had the Proverbs: 'Don't laugh when your enemy falls; don't crow over his collapse" (Prov. 24:17). When Jesus said, 'Love your enemies,' he added nothing to what this psalmist already had before him."[26]

But, Jesus brought the teaching of love to new heights of importance for His disciples. His way of showing love differed significantly from other rabbis. Remember that every disciple was expected to not only embrace the rabbi's teaching, but also his lifestyle. The following story helps bring this into focus:

> "The Talmud tells that a Gentile came to Shammai saying that he would convert to Judaism if Shammai could teach him the whole Torah in the time that he could stand on one foot. Shammai drove him away with a builder's measuring stick! Hillel, on the other hand, converted the Gentile by telling him,

'That which is hateful to you, do not do to your neighbor. That is the whole Torah; the rest is commentary. Go and study it.'"[27]

Notice that Hillel's "Golden Rule" was negative, emphasizing what NOT to do. Jesus put His Golden Rule in the positive, as does Leviticus, and taught His followers what to do. **"So in everything , do to others what you would have them do to you, for this sums up the law and the prophets"** (Matthew 7:12). Jesus was shocking in His love. He touched lepers. Ate with prostitutes. Blessed babies and invited children to gather around Him for teaching. Stayed overnight and feasted at the homes of infamous tax collectors. Delivered demoniacs. Healed the sick. His accessibility to and care for the multitudes was refreshingly different from other great rabbis.

A Very Different School of Love

Jesus did another thing that challenged Jewish practice. Unlike other sages of His day, He called everyone, including women and children. Jesus welcomed women! That made him very different. And highly controversial.

His door to discipleship was simply too large, as He invited all to follow Him. **"Come to me, all you who are weary and burdened, and I will give you rest. Take my yoke upon you and learn from me, for I am gentle and humble in heart, and you will find rest for your souls. For my yoke is easy and my burden is light"** (Matthew 11:28-30). One Hebrew expert, David Bivin, helps us understand these amazing words,

> "How would Jesus' first listeners have heard his words about taking on his yoke? ... In a rabbi-disciple relationship, the disciple wasexpected to place himself in a position of total obedience and dedication to his rabbi and his philosophy. It was his desire to become just like him. This was said to be taking on the "yoke" of the rabbi...Taking on a rabbi's yoke was not negative. When one's desire is to pull the same load as his teacher, the best way to do it is to willingly bind oneself to his yoke and cart."[28]

Jesus loved radically. And it is that yoke of love that He calls us to pull with Him. He commands His followers to bind themselves to doing the same acts of love that He did. That mark distinguished Him and His school from all others. Does love describe you?

How Love Looks

When discussing with "an expert of the law" how love to God and neighbor were the epitome of keeping the law, Jesus gave His famous parable of "the Good Samaritan." The legal expert "**wanted to justify himself**," so he asked Jesus, "**who is my neighbor?**" In His parable, Jesus identified a Jewish priest and a Levite, as those who "**passed by on the other side.**"

"But a Samaritan, as he traveled, came where the man was; and when he saw him, he took pity on him. He went to him andbandaged his wounds, pouring on oil and wine. Then he put theman on his own donkey, took him to an inn and took careof him. The next day he took out two silver coins and gave them to the innkeeper. 'Look after him,' he said, 'and when I return, I will reimburse you for any extra expense you may have.' Which

of these three do you think was a neighbor to the man who fell into the hands of the robbers? The expert in the law replied, 'The one who had mercy on him.' Jesus told him, 'Go and do likewise.'" (Luke 10:25-37)

Although they were obliged to teach on love, few of Jerusalem's rabbis distinguished themselves by loving as He loved. So, Jesus said to the crowds and to His disciples, **"The teachers of the law and the Pharisees sit in Moses' seat. So you must obey them and do everything they tell you. But do not do what they do, for they do not practice what they preach"** (Matthew 23:1-3). It was especially here, with His obvious life of selfless love, that His life and school were absolutely unique. And as it was then, so it should be now. Could we follow Jesus in this way? Or are we more like the unloving priest and rabbi than like the loving Samaritan?

Why Jesus Wins

"Love never fails." (1 Corinthians 13:8a). Love always leaves its mark and influences its recipients. Today there are thousands of new disciples who are following Jesus in love as He is saving them out of Islam and other forms of religious bondage. Where is Christ's love leading them? Jerry Trousdale shares some of their remarkable stories of love in his book, Miraculous Movements: How Hundreds of Thousands of Muslims are Falling in Love with Jesus. He concludes, "If you want to touch a Muslim's heart with the gospel, you have to be a genuine friend. You need to ask God to give you honest concern for them, not see Muslims as trophy conversions, but as people whom God loves and whom you can love as well."[29] Get Jerry's book and read how love is winning through these 21st century disciples of Jesus. Their testimonies of courageous, sacrificial love will help you to **"go and do likewise"** in your own context. If you want to win, then follow the Winner, Jesus. And love always wins!

An Ugly Heap

When Jesus taught that **"All the Law and the Prophets hang on these two commandments,"** (Matthew 22:40), He depicted love as the nail upon which all the rest of Scripture was to be displayed. Take the nail away from a beautiful picture hanging on the wall, and it crashes to the ground, losing its beauty and purpose. When we remove the "nail" of love from our handling of the Bible, it also crashes to the ground in an ugly heap. Our Christian lives are filled with such heaps—if we care to look and stop sweeping them under the rug. Countless relationships and opportunities that have never been developed because we were too focused on ourselves. **"Love never seeks its own"** (1 Cor. 13:5 – NKJV).

An Unforgettable Night

If you were to list the commands of God that matter most to you, would love be at the top of the list? It was at the top of Jesus' list and He passed on its preeminence clearly to His disciples. He chose to do so on an evening they would never forget. In the upper room, just before He was arrested and killed.

On that fateful night Jesus spoke of this one command. (The Lord Jesus used the formal word for command here that He and the Gospel writers use elsewhere of the commandments or laws of Moses.[30]) There is no question that Jesus wanted His disciples to approach love with the same care and devotion with which observant Jews approached the Ten Commandments. When Jesus used the word command, it was different from how others used that word. They had 613 commands and many more "fence laws" to keep them from breaking the 613 Scriptural laws. It was often the debate of these secondary commands or laws that became the focus of one rabbi's school diverging from other schools. Fence laws divided the Jews into distinctive and sometimes disruptive groups. The love law of Jesus was given to unite His disciples.

On the night He was betrayed, He issued one supreme command: to love one another. This command to love was especially what Jesus wanted to be the basis of everything He had communicated to them. Of all the many other commands He had issued and expected to be obeyed, this was given supremacy. See how clearly and repeatedly Jesus spoke of love during the hours when His life was drawing to its violent closure. We are amazed, as New Testament scholar, Leon Morris, noted, "The Greek noun agape ("love") and the verb *agapao* ("love") occur only 8 times in [John] chapters 1-12 but 31 times in chapters 13-17."[31]

Jesus said, **"A new command I give you: Love one another. As I have loved you, so you must love one another. By this all men will know that you are my disciples, if you love one another"** (John 13:34-35)[32]. He did not want us to forget this simple command. How could He have put it more clearly? Yet is this true of most of us? He clearly taught that love was the main proof of their discipleship.

Just as all professional sports teams dress all their players in the same colored uniforms, distinguishing them from other teams, so love is the clothing of Christ's true disciples. So we would never forget, He chose an unforgettable night and repeated the command several times that evening:

**Jesus replied, "<u>Anyone who loves me will obey my teaching.</u> My Father will love them, and we will come to them and make our home with them.
Anyone who does not love me will not obey my teaching. These words you hear**

are not my own; they belong to the Father who sent me.
(John 14:23-24)

As the Father has loved me, so have I loved you. Now <u>remain in my love</u>.
If you keep my commands, you will remain in my love, just as I have kept my Father's commands and remain in his love.
(John 15:9-10)

My command is this: Love each other as I have loved you. Greater love has no one than this: to lay down one's life for one's friends.
(John 15:12-13)

"I in them and you in me – so that they may be brought to complete unity. Then in the world will know that you sent me and have loved them even as you have loved me...

"I have made you known to them, and will continue to make you known in order that <u>the love you have for me may be in them and that I myself may be in them</u>."
(John 17:23, 26)

All Jesus' incredible wisdom given over several years is here reduced to **one** basic command. This is the one distinguishing sign written over the School of Jesus. It is like the carefully crafted slogan depicting one's business in a phrase. "Just do it." "America runs on Dunkin.'" "15 minutes will save you 15% on your car insurance." What was Jesus' slogan? What set His school apart from all others? **"Love one another."**

Do you better sense the importance of His love? Can't you feel the loss when love is absent, no matter what else is present? For me, this one command leads me constantly to repent of my sin. To love Him with every thought, emotion and deed demands everything. Whenever I hold back or misdirect my thoughts, emotions and actions, I am led back to Him, to my God of Love, by confessing my lack of love. I know, in that moment, I insanely have stopped following Jesus. Do I beat myself up? No! I trust in the perfectly obedient love of my Savior and in His dying love for me. Then I get up, realizing **"it is finished,"** through Christ and with true repentance follow Him again. I invite you, with me, to let His one great command to love frame your entire life inwardly and outwardly. I welcome you to **"Be imitators of God…and live**

a life of love, just as Christ loved us and gave himself for us as a fragrant offering and sacrifice to God" (Ephesians 5:1-2).

As we wind down this pivotal chapter, consider how Jesus' command to love is even more than we realized. Living a life of love is the very fingerprint of Jesus in the world today. Of all the ways He could choose to be identified in years and centuries to come, He chose love. It is His definitive mark. For all His disciples in all places on the earth, **"by this will all men know you are my disciples, if you love one another."** By His first disciples then and by His later disciples today, Jesus forever is to be known by His selfless love pouring through our lives to friend and foe alike. If we do not understand and embrace His love, we have removed from us the most distinguishing characteristic of the life of Christ, Himself.

When Love is Lost

The seriousness of getting love right has been forever etched into our consciousness by Christ's own words to the church at Ephesus. There He speaks of love's primacy, not as before, on the night of Gethsemane and the eve of His crucifixion. Not in weakness and weeping to those who were about to forsake Him and flee. No. Here the risen and reigning King of kings speaks to the Ephesians from heaven's throne. He solemnly warns us with the one clear command—to love!

"To the angel of the church in Ephesus write: These are the words of him who holds the seven stars in his right hand and walks among the seven golden lampstands. I know your deeds, your hard work and your perseverance. I know that you cannot tolerate wicked people, that you have tested those who claim to be apostles but are not, and have found them false. You have persevered and have endured hardships for my name, and have not grown weary. Yet I hold this against you: You have forsaken the love you had at first. Consider how far you have fallen! Repent and do the things you did at first. If you do not repent, I will come to you and remove your lampstand from its place" (Revelation 2:1-5).

Jesus would rather remove a significant church from the earth than have it live without its first love. Why? Christianity without love is a counterfeit. We were born again by a God of love to live a life of love.

In his unparalleled chapter on love (1 Corinthians 13), Paul begins by showing how we may **now** be **nothing** without love (13:1-3). And at its close (13:8-13), he reveals that Christ is leading us away from all that perishes into the greatest possible life—an endless existence of perfect love with Himself. As NT Wright so well explains,

> "The point of 1 Corinthians 13 is that love is not our duty, it is our destiny. It is the language Jesus spoke, and we are called to speak it so that we can converse with him. It is the food they eat in God's new world and we must acquire the taste for it here and now. It is the music God has written for all his creatures to sing, and we are called to learn and practice it now so as to be ready when the conductor brings down his baton. It is the resurrection life, and the resurrected

Jesus calls us to begin living it with him and for him right now."[33]

Love is now and will always be the greatest command of Jesus. It will never fail. It was love that "turned the world upside down"[34] in the 1st century and is doing so again in the 21st century.[35] Why not become or renew yourself as a disciple and let His love turn your world upside down, too?

We have concluded Part One. Do you think that we succeeded in identifying three main reasons why Christians rarely obey Jesus? We said they were:

(1) Because they have NOT seriously accepted the call to be true disciples;
(2) Because they exist in a Christian culture that no longer emphasizes obedience;
(3) Because they are NOT filled with the love of Jesus flowing in and from them by the Holy Spirit.

How would your life, your family and your church be changed if YOU responded to the Spirit TODAY in these three areas? You must decide for yourself. Don't wait. The world needs to see Christians whom they would call disciples of Jesus!

A 21st Century Disciple's Story

My name is Brewster. The hardest command for me to obey is the command *to die to myself*. I have served as a pastor in the same congregation for over 20 years and every time my wife and I try to leave, the Lord will not let us.

There have been several crises over this 20 plus years. Some deeply private; some occurring in a more public way involving my family; some concerning theological conflicts and spiritual battles in my denomination. Each prompted a season of intense desolation. And, I could always find someone to agree with me, nod the head and say, "Yes, it would be a good for you to take another call." Yet, as I would pursue viable options and get very close to choosing one, the Lord would get my attention and ask me to die to self and stay put.

Each occasion has been a painful submission and required yet another bruising of my pride, my willfulness, at times my anger, as well as my craving for novelty and the need to be energized by the next great thing.

Many people, my family and close friends included, were probably unaware of the interior struggle. The scene in which Jacob wrestles all night with the angel by the river Jabok became a friend. At the end of the day, God was asking me to die for the sake of His love for this people. He was conforming me to the image of His Son Jesus.

The result of obeying Jesus has been an amazing growth in Christ to me, my wife and our beloved congregation. Faithfulness has produced fruitfulness. But, please note, there is not stellar heroism here; just the ordinariness of saying, "Yes" to the Lord, each and every day.

I have been called to be like a cottage farmer, who contends with well-trod paths, thorns and thistles as well as stubborn rocks and fallow seasons. Our call is to tend the patch we are given as we trust the Sower who guarantees an infinite supply of seeds. And He always does, by His extravagant mercy, to those who stay and die. Come and join us as we follow Jesus.

Quote from Andrew Murray

"The deeper blessings of God's grace and the full enjoyment of God's love and nearness have been beyond our reach simply because obedience was never given the importance God gives it—the starting point and the goal of our Christian life." (16)

Questions for Reflection

1. Discuss how your view of the love of God has changed since reading this chapter.
2. Why is considering the Great Commandment such an effective way to convict us of sin and call us to repentance?
3. How does your life and your church measure up to the one-word command to love?
4. What forms might love take in you and your church IF your repentance is real?

5. Discuss Colossians 3:12-14; Ephesians 5:1-2 or 1 Peter 4:7-8

One-word Command to Obey

"Love"

But I tell you, **love** your enemies and pray for those who persecute you (Matthew 5:44)

"Jesus replied: '**Love** the Lord your God with all your heart and with all your soul and with all your mind.' This is the first and greatest commandment. And the second is like it: '**Love** your neighbor as yourself.'"

"A new command I give you: **Love** one another. As I have **loved** you, so you must **love** one another. By this everyone will know that you are my disciples, if you love one another." (John 13:34-35)

"If you **love** me, keep my commands. (John 14:15)

"As the Father has **loved** me, so have I **loved** you. Now remain in my **love.** (John 15:9)

My command is this: **Love** each other as I have **loved** you. (John 15:12)

This is my command: **Love** each other. (John 15:17)

When they had finished eating, Jesus said to Simon Peter, "Simon son of John, do you **love** me more than these?" "Yes, Lord," he said, "you know that I **love** you." Jesus said, "Feed my lambs." Again Jesus said, "Simon son of John, do you **love** me?" He answered, "Yes, Lord, you know that I **love** you." Jesus said, "Take care of my sheep." The third time he said to him, "Simon son of John, do you **love** me?" Peter was hurt because Jesus asked him the third time, "Do you **love** me?" He said, "Lord, you know all thing; you know that I love you." Jesus said, "Feed my sheep." (John 21:15-17)

"Then Jesus came to them and said, All authority in heaven and on earth has been given to me. Therefore, go and make disciples of all nations, baptizing them…and teaching them <u>to obey everything</u> I have commanded you. And surely I am with you to the end of the age" (Matthew 28:18-20)

"Knowledge without obedience creates a spiritual dichotomy between knowledge and obedience. This, tragically, is a toxic spiritual brew… Eve's sin was choosing knowledge over obedience and that same foolish choice plagues the modern church….Knowledge alone never produces spiritual growth and maturity because it doesn't transform life. Obedient discipleship does. The gold standard of discipleship is Jesus' own words: ***"Make disciples…teaching them to observe all things that I have commanded you"*** *(Matt 18:19,20).*

(Jerry Trousdale - Miraculous Movements, pp100-101)

"In baptism, it's more than the tobacco, the drinking and the gambling that stay under the water. It's self. People must understand that. When they come up out of the water, they leave themselves behind. They are completely finished. It's a totally new self which now begins to live a life of obedience, and this must be very plain.

(Juan Carlos Ortiz, Disciple, p53)

Part Two

How Jesus Obeyed

Chapter Four

Christ's *Passionate* Obedience

You have just read God's last, great command for His Church. A command to make disciples until Jesus returns at the end of the age. The words are crystal clear: **"teaching them to obey everything I have commanded you."** So, disciples made by the Great Commission do not merely obey generally. They obey specifically. Not picking and choosing what appeals to them or what might be convenient. Disciples are called to obey everything the Master demanded. And to pass that obedient way of life on until the age ends and He returns installing His Kingdom fully on earth. Something seems to have seriously gone wrong with this plan. We have dropped the ball and obedience to Jesus is no longer a hallmark of many who call themselves Christians.

When I first read the writings of 20th century disciple-pastor Juan Carlos Ortiz, they took my breath away! I could not believe what I was reading. Listen to this leader who not only wrote boldly, but bravely led his family and congregation in obeying all Christ's commands. And you, too, likely will be shocked.

> "The gospel we have in the Bible is the gospel of the Kingdom of God. It presents Jesus as King, as Lord, as the maximum authority. Jesus is the very center. The gospel of the Kingdom is a Christ-centered gospel…. Our gospel is like Aladdin's lamp; we think we can shake it and receive everything we like….
>
> "I am not just talking about semantics; I am talking about the tremendous attitude problem we have in the churches. It's not enough that we change our vocabularies; we must let God take out our brains, wash them in detergent, brush them and put them back in

the other way. Our whole set of values must be changed....

"But it is very hard to change. Even our motivation for evangelism is man-centered... We said, 'Poor people! Let's go and save them.' You see, we went not for Jesus' sake, but for lost souls' sake. That may look nice, but it's wrong, because everything must be Christ-motivated. We do not preach to lost souls because they are lost. We go to extend the Kingdom of God because God says so, and He is the Lord....

"Our modern gospel is what I call the Fifth Gospel. We have the gospels of Saints Matthew, Mark, Luke and John, and the Gospel according to Saint Evangelicals. The Gospel according to Saint Evangelicals is taken from verses here and there in the other four Gospels. We take all the verses we like, all the verses that offer something or promise something—John 3:16; John 5:24, and so forth—and we make a systematic theology from these verses, while we forget the other verses that present the demands of Jesus Christ. Who authorized that? Who said we are allowed to present only one side of Jesus?

"...I will give an example of the Fifth Gospel. Luke 12:32, "Fear not little flock, for it is your Father's good pleasure to give you the kingdom." But what about the next verse? "Sell your possessions and give to charity." I've never heard a sermon on this verse, because it is not in the Gospel according to the Saint Evangelicals. Verse 32 is part of our Fifth Gospel, but verse 33 is not—and it is a command from Jesus. Who has the right to decide which commandments are compulsory and which are optional? You see, the Fifth Gospel has made a strange thing: an optional commandment! You do it if you want; if you don't, that's all right, too. But that's not the gospel of the Kingdom."[36]

Let me continue with a couple probing questions: How can we consider ourselves to be His disciples if we do not reflect on His commands or obey them? Where did we ever get the idea that it was possible to be Christians who would have a legitimate relationship with Him while routinely disregarding what He commanded His followers to do?

Following or Stopping?

We need to go back to the beginning, as Ortiz recommended. The first recorded words in Mark's Gospel that Jesus spoke to Peter were these, **"Come, follow me...."** (Mk 1:17). The last recorded words in John's Gospel that Jesus spoke to Peter were these: **"If I want him to remain alive until I return, what is that to you. You must follow me."** (John 21:22). He began and ended His earthly relationship with Peter by the same two-worded command: Follow Me.

Michael Wilkins reminds us,

> "Following Jesus" is a technical expression for going after him as his disciple. The disciple is the one who has counted the cost, has made a commitment of faith, and has then "followed" Jesus... Some disciples physically followed Jesus around ... in his earthly ministry, while other disciples followed Jesus as

his disciples only in a figurative sense (Joseph – Jn 19:38).[37]

First and last words are especially important when they are the same. To repeat them the speaker must think they are basic, vital and enduring. So, to believers who walked with Jesus physically or for those wanting to follow Him long after His ascension into heaven, He speaks the same words—**"Follow Me."** But somewhere along the line millions of Christians have forgotten that those words demand obedience. When a Christians stops obeying, he stops following Jesus and, thus, stops being a disciple (see John 6:66). But even though many Christians have stopped obeying Jesus, if they ever started, they have remained as members in good standing in Christian churches. What was once unthinkable has become, sadly, the norm in many churches today. How can one be a disciple and a rebel at the same time? That is only possible where faith no longer is authenticated by a loving obedience. Disciple making pastor, Kyle Idleman, recently wrote,

> "If you read through the four Gospels that tell of Christ's life, you'll find that

Jesus says, 'Believe in me' about five times. But care to guess how many times Jesus said 'Follow me'? About twenty times. Now I'm not saying that following is more important than believing. What I am saying is that the two are firmly connected… To truly believe is to follow."[38]

Never forget that the call of Jesus, **"Follow me,"** is a call demanding immediate obedience. You cannot follow Jesus and stay where you are. You cannot follow Jesus and think about it for a while longer. When Jesus said, **"Follow me,"** there was instant response. Immediate movement. A new day. Response to His call takes your life in another direction. It is often stark and sudden.

When Matthew (Levi) was collecting taxes and Jesus stopped and called out to him, **"Follow me,"** the gospel states, **"Matthew got up and followed him"** (Matthew 9:9). Bonhoeffer rebukes the reasoning that concludes Matthew must have had other times to consider the call, because no one can reasonably be expected to just get up and walk away from his vocation,

"The call goes forth, and is at once followed by the response of obedience... Howcould the call immediately evoke obedience? ...For the simple reason that the cause behind the immediate following of the call is Jesus Christ himself. It is Jesus who calls, and because it is Jesus, Levi follows at once. This encounter is a testimony to the absolute, direct,and unaccountable authority of Jesus."[39]

The only way that humans should respond when God summons them, is to leave where they are and go where God tells them to go. Just as when God said, **"Let there be light, and there was light,"** so when Jesus calls, His sheep follow. **"My sheep listen to my voice. I know them, and they follow me"** (Genesis 1:3 then John 10:27).

In this chapter we lay the foundation for all future chapters by briefly looking at how Jesus obeyed. He is the perfect example of obedience. He obeys without a moment of disobedience, through terrible temptations and unspeakable sufferings. Jesus obeyed His Father being strengthened in His human nature by the complete filling of the Holy Spirit. So, we need the Spirit's constant help to follow God, too. The path is narrow and hard. But the reward is great and certain. So, **"Let us fix our eyes on Jesus, the author and perfecter of our faith, who for the joy set before him endured the cross, scorning its shame, and sat down at the right hand of the throne of God. Consider him who endured such opposition from sinful men, so that you will not grow weary and lose heart"** (Hebrews 12:2-3).

Please carefully consider the first way in which Jesus obeyed the Father. And as you fix your mind on Jesus, ask the Spirit to help you follow Him as He followed the Father. He promises to **"help us in our weakness"** (Romans 8:26).

Jesus Obeyed Wholeheartedly

How passionately do you want to obey God? David is recorded to have prayed, **"I desire to do your will, O my God; your law is within my heart"** (Psalm 40:8). We know that the heart is the place where we keep what we most cherish. As Jesus said, **"For where**

your treasure is, there your heart will be also" (Matthew 6:21). David's heart throbbed with desire to obey God's will. So did Christ's. He obeyed wholeheartedly. The author of Hebrews uses Psalm 40 as describing exactly what filled Jesus when He came into the world. **"Therefore, when Christ came into the world, he said: 'Here I am—it is written about me in the scroll—I have come to do your will, O God'"** (Hebrews 10:5-7). Even more so than David, Jesus hid God's Word in His heart as His treasure.

Help us, Spirit, to let go of what we treasure and make Christ's commands our desire and delight. The love of our hearts. Not because they are good, not because they are helpful, not because they will keep us out of trouble—but primarily because they are His commands. May we love everything about Him, mainly the words that He spoke. May all His Words, especially His commands, be kept like a treasure in our hearts and followed faithfully by our lives. Keep us from being halfhearted. Lukewarm.

Idleman reminds us of the passionate desire Jesus requires of His pursuers,

"In Luke 9:23 Jesus defines the relationship he wants with us. He makes it clear what it means to be a follower: 'If anyone would come after me, he must deny himself and take up his cross daily and follow me.' The phrase I want to draw your attention to is 'come after.' It's a phrase that was commonly used in the context of a romantic relationship. When Jesus says, 'Come after,' he's describing <u>a passionate pursuit</u> of someone you love. So the best way to understand what Jesus is wanting from us as followers is to compare how we pursue someone with whom we want to have a romantic relationship….

"I could tell you how I delivered furniture in the heat of the summer for minimum wage, but enjoyed it because the money was going for a wedding ring.… I could tell you how I donated plasma so I could buy her a dozen roses.… But you know, looking back at my relationship with Christ, I don't have as many stories about chasing after Jesus. The ones I could tell you hardly seem impressive enough to write down here"[40]

John repeatedly captured Christ's love for doing the Father's will in his Gospel. When Christ's disciples returned from fetching food in Samaria, they **"were surprised to find him talking with a woman…and urged him, 'Rabbi, eat something.' But he said to them, 'I have food to eat that you know nothing about.' Then his disciples said to each other, 'Could someone have brought him food?' Jesus said, 'My food, is to do the will of him who sent me and to finish his work'"** (John 4:27-34). The deep way that we crave for food when we are extremely hungry, Jesus craved to obey God's will. I know what it is to be famished and dive into a plate of food. Holy Spirit, help me to so hunger and long to fulfill the will of my Lord Jesus!

Jesus knew that His obedience "pleased" the Father (John 5:30). He said, **"For I have come down from heaven not to do my will but the will of him who sent me"** (John 6:38). Doing what someone else wants, when we would rather not, is often hard for us. Unless we really love the other person. Then listening to him or her and laying aside our own desires is not that hard. Love helps us submit to others. Jesus linked love for God with obedience of

God. When obedience is driven by love it is much more beautiful and powerful than that which is fueled by fear or obligation. On the night before His death, Jesus said,

"As the Father has loved me, so have I loved you. Now remain in my love. If you obey my commands, you will remain in my love, just as I have obeyed my Father's commands and remain in his love. I have told you this so that my joy might be in you and that your joy might be complete" (John 15:9-11).

Notice how Jesus obeyed with desire, love and joy. How often do we see obedience, love and joy linked in Christians' lives today? Think of something that excites you and stirs your heart. A ball game. A family reunion. An election that turns out the way we hoped. A beautiful day at the shore. How often do you obey God with that same excitement? How many times have love and obedience captured our hearts—at the same time? May God have mercy and help us in our weakness. Fill us, dear Spirit, with the joy of a loving obedience to Jesus!

A 21ˢᵗ Century Disciple's Story

My name is Jeff. When Jesus renewed my call to follow Him, the hardest obedience He demanded was ... *my time*. I am by nature a comfort seeker who enjoys when I have plenty of time without responsibility or accountability.

Also, being "churched" for all of my life, it was easy to compartmentalize my time and obedience to Him. This restricted His call on my life to Sunday mornings and maybe even Sunday evenings or a weekday Bible study. Though being a leader in a church, there was little consequence for my not giving all my time to the work of His kingdom. I and others saw me as doing much more than many others, so why do more? But I learned through biblical discipleship that Jesus doesn't ask for just "more than some other people". He asks for it all.

And this has been the result of my obeying Jesus…that I am busier than ever but have never felt so free to give of my coveted, "me" time. My obeying Jesus has taken the form of more time spent in prayer, more time spent in the Word, more time connecting with and serving others, more time just thinking about

Him and other people, all the while realizing how much more time I could give and how I'm only scratching the surface. By His grace, He has been patient with me as I timidly and imperfectly take each step to follow Him. He has reminded me that I am not my own and that my life is to be spent serving Him and serving others. What I am finding is that even with baby steps towards that end, the blessings of joy and hope and faith are being given to me in abundance. Come and follow Jesus with us.

Quote from Andrew Murray

"How often and how earnestly we have asked how to abide more continually in Christ. We have imagined that more study of the Word, more faith, more prayer, or more communion with God would surely be the keys, but we have overlooked a simple truth: 'He who has my commandments and keeps them loves Me.' So again, obedience is the key." (17-18)

Disciples OBEY

Questions for Reflection

1. What do you think of Ortiz's "Gospel of Saint Evangelicals?" Does he have a valid point? Is this a serious flaw or a slight flaw in your mind?
2. Describe today's normal Christian life and compare it with "following Jesus."
3. Discuss what Idleman says about "going after" or pursuing Jesus. Do you have any stories of your passionate pursuit or is your relationship with Jesus not much to brag about?
4. Discuss the link between loving God and obeying God.

One-phrase Command to Obey

"Follow Me"

"Como, **follow me,**" Jesus said, "and I will send you out to fish for people." (Matthew 4:19)

But Jesus told him, "**Follow me,** and let the dead bury their own dead." (Matthew 8:22)

As Jesus went on from there, he saw a man named Matthew sitting at the tax collector's booth. **"Follow me,"** he told him, and Matthew got up and **followed** him. (Matthew 9:9)

Whoever does not take up their cross and **follow me** is not worthy of me. (Matthew 10:38)

Then Jesus said to his disciples, "Whoever wants to be my disciple must deny themselves and take up their cross and **follow me.** (Matthew 16:24)

Jesus answered, "If you want to be perfect, go, sell your possessions and give to the poor, and you will have treasure in heaven. Then come, **follow me.**" (Matthew 19:21)

Peter answered him, "We have left everything to **follow** you! What then will there be for us? Jesus said to them, "Truly I tell you, at the renewal of all things, when the Son of Man sits on his glorious throne, you who have **followed me** will also sit on twelve thrones, judging the twelve tribes of Israel. (John 19:27-28)

The next day Jesus decided to leave for Galilee. Finding Philip, he said to him, **"Follow me."** (John 1:43)

When Jesus spoke again to the people he said, "I am the light of the world. Whoever **follows me** will never walk in the darkness, but will have the light of life." (John 10:27)

Whoever serves me must **follow me**; and where I am, my servant also will be. My Father will honor the one who serves me. (John 12:16)

Jesus said this to indicate the kind of death by which Peter would glorify God. Then he said to him, **"Follow me!"** (John 21:19)

Jesus answered, "If I want him to remain alive until I return, what is that to you? You must **follow me."** (John 21:22)

"Jesus said to them ... He who is not with me is against me, and he who does not gather with me scatters." (Matthew 12:32)

"While Jesus was still talking to the crowd, his mother and brothers stood outside, wanting to speak to him. Someone told him, "Your mother and brothers are standing outside, wanting to speak to you." He replied to him, "Who is my mother, and who are my brothers?" Pointing to his disciples, he said, "Here are my mother and my brothers. For whoever does the will of my Father in heaven is my brother and sister and mother." (Matthew 12:46-50)

"Matthew intends for his readers to understand that the Christian life is equivalent to being with Jesus as his disciple. This means that conversion—not a later point of commitment...marks the beginning point of discipleship. Degrees of maturity will be realized as one traverses the discipleship path, but all true believers are disciples on that path....Obedience to Jesus' teaching is the heart of discipleship training and it is the calling for all believers."

(Michael Wilkins, Following the Master, pp191-192)

"Beware of the carnal appetites of the body. If someone strikes you on the right cheek, turn the other one to him as well.... Should anyone compel you to go a mile, go another one with him....If someone takes away your coat, let him have your shirt too. If someone seizes anything belonging to you, do not ask for it back again....Give to everyone that asks, without looking for repayment, for it is the Father's pleasure that we should share His gracious bounty with all men. A giver who

gives freely, as the commandment directs, is blessed; no fault can be found with him. But woe to the taker....See that you do not neglect the commandments of the Lord, but keep them just as you received them, without any additions or subtractions of your own."

(The Didache or Teaching of the Apostles, ca 90AD - 1:1, 4)

Chapter Five

Christ's *Presence* Obedience

How real is God's presence to you throughout the day? Three great believers featured in Genesis were Enoch, Noah and Abraham. The account states that both Enoch and Noah **"walked with God"** (Genesis 5:22; 6:9). Genesis also states, **"When Abraham was ninety-nine years old, the Lord appeared to him and said, "I am God Almighty, <u>walk before me</u>…."** (Genesis 17:1). God's command to Abraham was that he should live "before God" or in God's presence. The book of Hebrews speaks of all three men and reminds us that they lived **"by faith"** (Hebrews 11:5, 7, 8, 11, 17). They did not do what they did because they saw God with their eyes. No, they obeyed God by faith. The same way you and I must obey, because Jesus is not physically with us. How often does your faith prompt you to remember and obey one of Jesus' clear commands?

Jesus lived in the presence of God. Think of what it would be like to hear someone actually speaking of the presence of God like Jesus did:

"I tell you the truth, the Son can do nothing by himself; he can only do what he sees his Father doing, because Whatever the Father does the Son also does" (John 5:19).

"The one who sent me is with me; he has not left me alone, for I always do what pleases him" (John 8:29).

"Do not believe me unless I do what my Father does. But if I do it, even though you do not believe in me, believe the miracles, that you may know and understand that the Father is in me, and I am in the Father." (John 10:37-38).

"So whatever I say is just what the Father has told me to say" (John 12:50b).

"Don't you believe that I am in the Father and the Father is in me? The words I say to you are not just my own. Rather, it is the Father, living in me, who is doing his work" (John 14:10).

Jesus Lived by Faith, too

We could easily forget that Jesus' walk was also by faith and not by sight. Although Jesus depended upon His Father every moment, God was not physically beside Him. As the Son of Man, Christ was fully man and obeyed as humans obey. But, unlike us, faith was complete or perfect in Him. So, He spoke of God as if He could see and talk with Him. As if God held constant, audible communication with Him. But He didn't. God remained a Spirit, ever with Him, but not physically so. What Enoch and Noah did occasionally and imperfectly, Jesus did constantly and perfectly. He walked with God by a faith that was burning with love.

Recently, while teaching the book of Acts, I discovered one of the clearest ways that the disciples in Acts differ from Christians now. *They lived in the presence of Jesus.* They acknowledged Him in their daily lives. They lived as if they knew Him. We live as if we know about Him. That is the BIG difference between present reality and past history. Do you live day by day as if Jesus was right there with you? Or is He only seated at God's right hand to you? Light years away from you?

"I am with you always" – Truth or Fiction?

My premise is simply this—that most Christians TODAY are NOT living in the presence of Jesus as our predecessors did in the Book of Acts. This impacts us and affects our response to His commands. The book of Acts begins with Jesus ascending into heaven while the disciples were watching. Two celestial beings asked them why they were looking into the skies, reminding them that Jesus promised He would return. Then they left them, too. So, what were the apostles of Jesus to do? Their Savior, Leader and God had ascended to heaven. They were left on earth among enemies who had just killed Jesus and remained rabidly opposed to them as His followers. Here were their basic options.

1. Run for their lives
2. Go underground until He returns to rescue them
3. Believe and obey what He has recently commanded them to do until He returns

So what did they choose? Thankfully, Luke records, **"Then they returned to Jerusalem from the hill called the Mount of Olives ... to the room where they were staying"** (Acts 1:12-13). There they waited for ten days until they were filled and empowered by the Holy Spirit. Where was Jesus while they were waiting? Where is Jesus today? Was Jesus with them in that upper room or was He totally apart from them in heaven? Are we living in a totally different era than theirs? Aren't we all still waiting for His return and committed to fulfilling His Great Commission as they were? Didn't He promise to them and us, "**And surely I am with you always, to the very end of the age**"?

Have you been taught that you are a different people, with a different task than the people on whom the Spirit fell on the Day of Pentecost? Probably not! Most every part of the Church today sees itself as ONE with them. Their history is our history. The epistles that the apostles and others wrote to those living at that time are written for us, too.

So, here is my question for you—are you walking in obedience to Jesus or have you run for your lives and gone underground waiting for His return? By the way, going to a Christian church that ignores obedience may be virtually the same as going underground. Here are some very challenging words from one who has long chosen to live in the presence of Jesus:

> "What was it like to constantly live in the presence of Christ? One thing is sure: it had radically transformed these twelve men. There were no other men like them on the earth. Certainly no one else could say as they did, "I have spent 20,000 hours living, breathing and walking in the presence of Jesus Christ.'

"...Just look at what 20,000 hours with Christ did to those 12 men: it purified them in motive, in deed and in thought. Probably we have never seen men so pure in heart, so purged of hidden motives....

"So what were the 12? ...They were men who lived in the conscious presence ofChrist. Furthermore, the Apostles had developed a habit during over three years with Jesus—the habit of always being in the Lord's presence—and they kept the habit even after He ascended! Is that impossible? No, it is experiencing that same intimate relationship with Christ. They were still living in His presence."[41]

In your Name or in Jesus' Name?

Here are some vital facts about Jesus and Acts that will help you live in His presence today. The name of Jesus is found over 70 times in Acts. He is mentioned or alluded to in every chapter of the book. Believers saw their lives connected with His and so, they did everything in His name. The phrase, "name of Jesus" is mentioned 18 times in the book. In chapter 19, seven brothers were trying to cast out a demon from a man by using the name of Jesus like a formula. They said, **"In the name of Jesus whom Paul preaches, I command you to come out."** The demon-afflicted man overpowered and beat them severely, saying, **"Jesus I know—and I know about Paul but who are you?"** The Ephesians **"were all seized with fear, and the name of the Lord Jesus was held in high honor"** (Acts 19:17).

Think about that, a whole city gripped by fear. One may be momentarily frightened by a sound, a shadow or a thought. But we do not live in fear of something that does not exist, of what is not a real and present threat. The world of the first century learned through the disciples of the first century that the Jesus they followed was a power to be reckoned with. All power had been given to Him, making Him King of kings and Lord of lords. They often invoked His name in what they were doing. How often do we actually say "in the name of Jesus" before doing something?[42] One reason that our Western cultures do not now recognize Christ's power is because we are not living in His presence and following Him as the first disciples did!

In Acts, Jesus is often recorded as really present with the disciples. Jesus chooses Judas' successor, calls and adds to the church those being saved, is seen by Stephen, by Paul and Peter. He strikes Elymas the Sorceror with blindness, and commands Paul and Barnabas to go to the Gentiles.[43] Luke represents Jesus as the One who opened Lydia's heart, spoke to Paul in a vision and encouraged him to stay in Corinth.[44] He appeared to Paul in a vision in the temple and later stood near Paul and said, **"Take courage! As you have testified about me in Jerusalem, so you must also testify in Rome."**[45] Luke did not present his history of the Early Church like Jesus was isolated in heaven, but as daily present with His people.

Since Jesus is present in Acts, we are not surprised to find that there is a strong emphasis on obeying God in Acts. When people live in the presence of God, they tend to obey God. Distance encourages disobedience. When called in to court by the same men who orchestrated Jesus' crucifixion, Peter and John said, **"Judge for yourselves whether it is right in God's sight to obey you rather than God. For we cannot help speaking about what we have seen and heard"** (Acts

4:19-20). And when describing the growth of the Jerusalem Church, Luke wrote, **"So the word spread. The number of disciples in Jerusalem increased rapidly, and a large number of priests became <u>obedient to the faith</u>"** (Acts 6:7). The faith of those converted Jewish priests was marked by obedience. How is your faith marked? How near is Jesus to you? How often do you call on His name or worship Him during the day? If your answer is, "occasionally" or "hardly at all," you are not living as His early disciples lived. But that can change! By the power of the Spirit, you can live by faith in Christ's presence as the first century disciples did. Edwards reminds us,

> "This deep fellowship of His presence was the mainstay of the early church.... Can you imagine what it would be like to live all the time with people who had but one desire—to know Christ, to know Him personally, to know Him intimately and to live in His presence?"[46]

Practice the Presence of God

Jesus lived in the presence of God. At Lazarus' tomb, **"Jesus looked up and said,**

'Father, I thank you that you heard me. I knew that you always hear me..." (John 11:41-42). Do you believe that Jesus always hears you when you talk to Him? You should. Is what was true of Jesus, true of us? Are you walking with God? Though Jesus was and is seated at the right hand of God on high, He is also really with His people. He identifies Himself as the One who **"walks among the seven golden lampstands"** (which are the seven churches of Asia- Revelation 1:20; 2:1). He never leaves or forsakes us. But are we forsaking Him? I have met thousands of Christians, but very few disciples who consciously follow Him every step throughout the day. There are few who could write what a simple servant named Brother Lawrence, wrote a few centuries ago,

> "...I renounced, for the love of Him, everything that was not He, and I began to live as if there was none but He and I in the world.... I made this my business as much all the day long as at the appointed times of prayer; for at all times, every hour, every minute, even in the height of my business, I drove away from my mind everything that

was capable of interrupting my thought of God"[47]

In his second letter, Brother Lawrence humbly noted,

"I make it my business only to persevere in His holy presence, wherein I keep myself by a simple attention, and a general fond regard to God, which I may call an actual presence of God; or, to speak better, an habitual, silent, and secret conversation of the soul with God, which often causes me joys… inwardly…so great that I am forced to use means to moderate them and prevent their appearance to others.

"…As for my set hours of prayer, they are only a continuation of the same exercise. Sometimes I consider myself there as a stone before a carver, whereof he is to make a statue; presenting myself thus before God, I desire Him to form His perfect image in my soul, and make me entirely like Himself"[48]

The biographer of Brother Lawrence represented his practicing God's presence as follows:

> "When he began his business, he said to God, 'O my God, since You are with me, and I must now, in obedience to Your commands, apply my mind to these outward things, I beseech You to grant me the grace to continue in Your presence; and to this end do prosper me with Your assistance, receive all my works, and possess all my affections. And when he had finished he examined himself how he had discharged his duty; if he found well, he returned thanks to God; if otherwise, he asked pardon, and, without being discouraged, he set his mind right again, and continued his exercise of the presence of God as if he had never deviated from it. 'Thus,' he said, 'by rising after my falls, and by frequently renewed acts of faith and love, I am come to a state wherein it would be as difficult for me not to think of God as it was at first to accustom myself to think of Him.'"[49]

Following or Orbiting?

When I came to faith, one of the first Bible texts I was told to memorize was Proverbs 3:5-6. **"Trust in the Lord with all your heart and lean not on your own understanding; in all your ways acknowledge him, and he will make your paths straight."** So, I memorized it. But the only people I saw doing what those verses said were new believers, like my parents. They seemed to obey the Word until they started going to church! When they got into the rhythm of Christian life with other believers they learned not to take the commands quite so literally. Instead, we learned how to use our own understanding and that we really did not need to acknowledge Jesus in everything. We were taught to live the normal Christian life.

You see, most of us are taught in church how to orbit around Jesus rather than how to follow Him step by step. We are shown how to live for Him like other good Christians do: daily Bible reading and prayer, going to church on Sunday and to youth and prayer meetings weekly. But what about the other days and hours? The disciples in Acts walked by faith with Jesus. I learned how to check in with Him in the morning and at meals and when I went to bed. Now I see that the difference between what I learned at church from Christians and what I had memorized in the Word is the difference between experiencing Christianity and living in the presence of Christ. I was taught how to be a good Christian (Baptist and Presbyterian), instead of being a faithful disciple of Jesus.

How thankful I am that my parents refused to be orbitized and continued to follow Jesus radically, though imperfectly, all their days. My dad went from being a dentist in New York to being a dental missionary in Africa. My mom is still a missionary in Florida. I saw my parents sell their possessions and leave the friends they loved, to follow Jesus. The security of wealth and a large house were gladly exchanged for living by faith in a mobile home. Some thought my parents had gone mad. I thought and still think that they were simply led by love to obey the command of Jesus to **"Go into all the world"** (Mark 16:15a). The reality and memory of their love and obedience have helped me not to get institutionalized or denominationalized—but rather, to follow Jesus. How will you be remembered?

A 21ˢᵗ Century Disciple's Story

My name is Tom. When Jesus renewed my call to follow Him, the hardest obedience He demanded was *asking me to enter into close relationships with others.*

My childhood was broken as I had no father figure in my life. Our family did not exchange hugs, words of encouragement or outward expressions of love. I was always told to protect myself from any harm by maintaining this defensive mode. So, when talking, I would only talk about general stuff. Nothing personal.

But this has been the result of my obeying Jesus. I have been involved in leading group prayer and during these times I have been able to share my personal testimony without guilt and shame. I opened my home to men who were in transition and needed temporary housing. While these men were living with me we shared our lives with one another and developed close relationships.

I came to realize that we need each other on a daily basis for support and accountability. In obeying Jesus, He has expanded my circle of friends into an extended family that now goes into several other areas of the city. I am part of a group called "On The Street Church" which meets Tuesdays and Fridays to share our struggles and be supportive in prayer and action. I am joining other disciples for intercessory prayer 6 different times a week, often taking the lead.

The Lord is truly healing my brokenness as I obey His command to love one another. I am learning that you cannot love others at a distance or without developing close relationships with them. Won't you embrace an intimate relationship with Jesus and follow Him with us?

Quote from Andrew Murray

"Just as we have trusted Him as our Savior to atone for our disobedience, let us trust Him as our teacher to lead us out of it and into a life of practical obedience. It is the presence of Christ with us throughout each day that will

keep us on the path of true commitment to our task." (43)

Questions for Reflection

1. When have you really felt the presence of Jesus in your life? Why do you think that this is **not** more common to you and other Christians?
2. How often do you say or act, "in the name of Jesus" during the day? Why so much or little?
3. Could you explain to someone else how to practice the presence of God? If so or if not, what does that reflect about your Christian upbringing?
4. Discuss the difference between orbiting around Jesus and following Him. List some of the elements of your church's or denomination's orbit (tradition)?

One-word command to Obey

"Pray"

But I tell you, love your enemies and **pray** for those who persecute you… (Matthew 5:44)

But when you **pray,** go into your room, close the door and **pray** to your father, who is unseen. Then you Father, who sees what is done in secret, will reward you. And when you **pray,** do not keep on babbling like pagans, for they think they will be heard because of their many words. (Matthew 6:6-7)

Watch and **pray** so that you will not fall into temptation. The spirit is willing, but the flesh is weak. (Matthew 26:41)

Pray that this will not take place in winter (Mark 13:18)

One day Jesus was **praying** in a certain place. When he finished, one of his disciples said to him, "Lord, teach us to **pray,** just as John taught his disciples." He said to them, "When you **pray,** say: "Father, hallowed be your name, Your kingdom come." (Luke 11:1-2)

The Jesus told his disciples a parable to show them that they should always **pray** and not give up. (Luke 18:1)

Be always on the watch, and **pray** that you may be able to escape all that is about to happen, and that you may be able to stand before the Son of Man. (Luke 21:36)

"Large crowds were traveling with Jesus, and turning to them he said: "If anyone comes to me and does not hate father and mother, wife and children, brothers and sisters—yes, even their own life—such a person cannot be my disciple. And whoever does not carry their cross and follow me cannot be my disciple. "Suppose one of you wants to build a tower. Won't you first sit down and estimate the cost to see if you have enough money to complete it? For if you lay the foundation and are not able to finish it, everyone who sees it will ridicule you, saying, 'This person began to build and wasn't able to finish.' ...In the same way, those of you who do not give up everything you have cannot be my disciples." (Luke 14:25-33)

"With such a call to a life of total and uncompromising obedience, we should not be surprised if we are strongly tempted to qualify Christ's call, to modify its stringent demands by taking a more "reasonable" line in the light of modern culture, which we tell ourselves, is "so different from that of the 1ˢᵗ century."

(David Watson, Discipleship, p234)

"Very likely your religion costs you nothing. Very probably it neither costs you trouble, nor time, nor thought, nor care, nor pains, nor reading, nor praying, nor self-denial, nor conflict, nor working, nor labor of any kind….Such a religion as this will never save your soul…A religion which costs nothing is worth nothing."

(Bishop JC Ryle in James Boice's Christ's Call to Discipleship, p112)

Chapter Six

Christ's *Perfect* Obedience

We live so easily with so much sin and imperfection that it might not deeply impress us that Jesus was morally perfect. He never sinned. We lean so hard on God's grace, too, that we sometimes wrongly shrug off both our and others' sins as no big deal. Almost everything today can be excused by saying, "You know, I'm only human." In fact, we have a natural suspicion of people who seem too-good-to-be-true. Who smile too often or don't ever get upset enough to blurt out an expletive.

But God really hates sin. Of course, hatred with God is different from hatred with us. Nevertheless, He is opposed to it. It offends

His nature and cannot be merely overlooked. The sacred Book which alone reveals how sinners may be saved, also declares that

"There are six things the Lord hates, seven that are detestable to him: Haughty eyes, a lying tongue, hands that shed innocent blood, a heart that devises wicked schemes, feet that are quick to rush into evil, a false witness who pours out lies and a man that stirs up dissension among brothers" (Proverbs 6:16-19).

Would it surprise you to think that Jesus hates these things, too?

Why Leviticus is such a Drag

When we start to read through the Bible in a year, we do okay until we get to Leviticus. It is so depressing. Why do you think Leviticus bores us? Maybe it is because sin is mentioned around 100 times in that book. The book is full of bloody, sin offerings. Bulls, sheep, lambs, rams and doves all have to die. Why? Because Israel was so full of sin. When reading it, we feel like throwing our hands up and crying,

Enough! And, unfortunately, more often than not, we miss the point.

"Your eyes are too pure to look on evil; you cannot tolerate wrong" (Habakkuk 1:13). **"Surely the arm of the Lord is not too short to save, nor his ear too dull to hear. But your iniquities have separated you from your God; your sins have hidden his face from you, so that he will not hear"** (Isaiah 59:1-2). We have almost forgotten **"the law requires that nearly everything be cleansed with blood, and without the shedding of blood there is no forgiveness"** (Hebrews 9:22).

We are sinners. And sin is the cause of all the evil, brokenness, war and death throughout the world. People like us are the cause of the world's woe. But Jesus was **"the Lamb of God, who takes away the sin of the world!"** (John 1:29). And as the lambs to be sacrificed had to be without defect, so was Jesus.

"When anyone brings from the herd or flock a fellowship offering, it must be without defect or blemish to be acceptable. Do not offer to the Lord

the blind, the injured or the maimed, or anything with warts or festering or running sores. Do not place any of these upon the altar as an offering made to the Lord by fire.... Keep my commands and follow them. I am the Lord. Do not profane my holy name. I must be acknowledged as holy by the Israelites. I am the Lord who makes you holy and who brought you out of Egypt to be your God. I am the Lord" (Leviticus 22:21-22, 31-33).

If Jesus had not lived perfectly, He would have been condemned as well. **"For the wages of sin is death"** (Romans 6:23a). He died only because He took upon Himself our sin and the death we deserved. He did not die for any lack in Himself. He suffered and died for you and me.

As Goes Sin, so Goes the Savior

Sin is serious stuff. But we live in a light and frivolous age. We like to laugh and try to keep from being too serious most of the time. Could it be that the gospel of Jesus, the good news of life through Him, does not seem so good today because we view sin as not being so bad any longer? How good is a remedy if it arrives just in time to save those who don't really need it? Wherever God's people retain the truth of sin's destructiveness, there remains room for the awesome beauty of Christ's sinlessness. But where sin is easily excused, sinlessness seems unremarkable. A low view of sin produces a low need for its remedy. And so, today, the gospel is reduced to merely a message for escaping hell rather than the good news of God's complete redemption of a fallen creation through the perfect Lamb of God.

Jesus had to be concerned about fulfilling the commands or laws of God, because it was the transgressing of those laws that created our dilemma in the first place. We might think little of sin. A just and holy God cannot. So, the public ministry of Jesus was begun by a baptism that was designed **"to fulfill all righteousness"** (Matthew 3:15). As such, His baptism was seen as part of the righteous requirements placed on Him by the righteous demands of God's law. Every step He took had to do with the Law of God His Father. So, Matthew's record of His life uses words like **"this was to fulfill what was spoken through**

the prophet" fifteen times.[50] Jesus' life was the fulfillment of both the demands and the promises of the Law and the Prophets.

A Sin-Concerned Life

Following His baptism, Jesus was then quickly **"led by the Spirit into the wilderness to be tempted by the devil"** (Matthew 4:1). He was tempted to sin. The satanic temptation that the first Adam did not endure, the second Adam, perfectly resisted and rejected (1 Corinthians 15:45). As the author of Hebrews so well put it, **"For we do not have a high priest who is unable to sympathize with our weaknesses, but we have one who has been tempted in every way, just as we are—yet without sin"** (Hebrews 4:15). The most careful keepers of the Law, could not keep the commands of God well enough, for Jesus said, **"unless your righteousness surpasses that of the Pharisees and the teachers of the law, you will certainly not enter the kingdom of heaven"** (Matthew 5:20). He was different from them. He could look His opponents straight in the eyes and ask them what they could never ask of others: **"Can any of you prove me guilty of sin?"** (John 8:46).

The sinlessness of Jesus is much more than merely a fine theological point. It is an historic reality of tremendous practical importance to every believer and the whole creation. **"For God was pleased to have all his fullness dwell in him, and through him to reconcile to himself all things, whether things on earth or things in heaven, by making peace through his blood, shed on the cross"** (Colossians 1:19-20). The salvation of a sin-laden creation is only possible through a sinless, risen Savior.

Paul again expressed the importance of this truth and wrote, **"God made him who had no sin to be sin for us, so that in him we might become the righteousness of God"** (2 Corinthians 5:21). Righteousness apart from Jesus is impossible. The righteousness of God is a free gift that is conveyed to believers by faith in Jesus, our righteous and sinless One. **"For in the gospel, a righteousness from God is revealed, a righteousness that is by faith from first to last.... This righteousness from God comes through faith in Jesus Christ to all who believe"** (Romans 1:17; 3:21). In other words, the perfect obedience of Jesus to the whole Law of God has been credited to us who have been saved by faith in Him.

"Do this and you shall live"

Something that neither we nor any Jewish leader could do, Jesus has done. He obeyed everything perfectly. He had to do this for us because, as Paul wrote, **"Cursed is everyone who does not continue to do everything written in the Book of the Law"** (Galatians 3:10 quoting Deuteronomy 27:26). Eternal life results from perfectly keeping the Law of God. **"The man who does these things shall live by them"** (Galatians 3:12). Since none of us are righteous, we needed a Righteous One who did what we cannot do, and thereby merited eternal life for us. He obeyed and we gain from His obedience. He died and His blood or life was the price paid for our redemption. This salvation is all by God's gracious love. It is such good news that it leaves us astounded and forever humbled, filled with immense gratitude.

As a result of our faith in Christ, we are included in the family of God and have been given a right to all the privileges of God's children! John marveled, **"How great is the love the Father has lavished on us, that we should be called children of God! And that is what we are!"** (1 John 3:1). We are **"children born not of natural descent, nor of human decision or a husband's will, but born of God"** (John 1:13).

Like Father like Sons

God's children, those born of God, resemble God. Jesus pressed this point when He taught about love. Read carefully what He said,

> **"You have heard that it was said, 'Love your neighbor and hate your enemy.' But I tell you, love your enemies and pray for thosewho persecute you, that you may be children of your Father in heaven. He causes his sun to rise on the evil and the good, and sends rain on the righteous and the unrighteous. If you love those who love you, what reward will you get? Are not even the tax collectors doing that? And if you greet only your own people, what are you**

doing more than others? Do not even pagans do that? Be perfect, therefore, as your heavenly Father is perfect." (Matthew 5:43-48)

We thank God that Jesus loved perfectly. All of our imperfect feelings and acts of love are forgiven through faith in Him. But being imperfect is no excuse for us to adopt any other way of life than love. NT Wright beautifully reminds us,

> "Jesus, at his ascension, was given by the creator God an empire built on love. As we ourselves open our lives to the warmth of that love, we begin to lose our fear; and as we begin to lose our fear, we begin to become people through whom the power of that love can flow out into the world around that so badly needs it. That is an essential part of what it means to follow Jesus. And as the power of that love replaces the love of power, so in a measure, anticipating the last great day, God's kingdom comes, and God's will is done on earth as it is in heaven. We will not see the work accomplished

in all its fullness until the last day. But we will, in following Jesus, be both implementing his work and hastening that day."⁵¹

Disciples obey. And the marks of obedience that matter most to us are those that mattered most to Jesus. We have seen that His obedience was perfectly filled with love for the ever-present Father. So, our aim and prayer is to walk with <u>the ever-present Jesus</u> in a life <u>of selfless love empowered by H</u>is Spirit. Though perfection is not attainable now, it is our desire. We can surely say with Paul, **"So I strive always to keep my conscience clear before God and man."** (Acts 24:16).

Unlike His perfect obedience, ours is always flawed. So, it is a Christ-exalting, faith-based obedience that we embrace and promote. One that is marked not so much by stress and strain as by sincerity. Following Jesus, we should find ourselves wholeheartedly in places and with people whom He loved to serve and help.

As Kyle Idleman reminds us,

> "The most literal way to define a 'Follower of Jesus' is 'Someone who goes where Jesus goes.' I'm not sure how you can call yourself a follower of Jesus if you refuse to go where Jesus went. If you are following Jesus 'wherever,' he will take you towards a sinner that others wouldn't want to be seen with."[52]

In Part Two we have seen that Jesus' obedience always exuded passion, presence and perfection. Our obedience, helped by His Spirit, should reflect a similar reality because following Him means following the way He lived. And this is our confidence—what our obedience lacks in passion, presence and perfection, His righteousness perfects and allows the Father to receive them as a pleasing aroma. What grace! May Jesus Christ, alone, be praised.

A 21ˢᵗ Century Disciple's Story

My name is John. When Jesus renewed my call to follow Him, the hardest obedience He demanded of me was ...*to Go!*

I needed to take time to be available (mostly to listen to people) and then talk with those who are "worthy." It seemed to me that people were most willing to talk when I seemed to be the busiest. I had to be patient and listen, realizing that I needed to learn (1) to do less and (2) to trust God with whatever was left undone.

And this has been the result of my obeying Jesus. I have my own business and two of us were working to meet a deadline of getting a house prepped to be sold. When I was working on the outside of the house, a neighbor came over and asked if I could help him with a small 30 minute job on his house.

I realized I would be able to have a conversation with him while I was working so I agreed.

He talked the entire time I was working, and really began to open up and share a serious problem he was having with his 20 year old son. The conversation continued for another hour or so. I found out that he had lost his job and yet had major expenses concerning his son's difficulties. A week later I heard from a friend about a company that was hiring so when I was working in the man's area again I went by his home to tell him about that company. While I was there I learned more about him and some other areas of his life that indicated great need. I made a few comments about God and he said that I reminded him of his father. That was when I learned about his upbringing in a home where the Bible was honored, yet he had turned his back on it.

Another time, I was again working near his home and he was outside and close enough that I could hear him and his neighbor in a conversation. When there was a break I waved and said hello and commented on the beautiful sky that we were blessed to enjoy. They both agreed. I came closer and he introduced me to his neighbor and I joined their conversation.

This is the beginning of a relationship that will soon see me asking the following question. "How would you like to discover for yourself what God is like and how He wants you to live?" I am so glad I took the time to GO! Won't you follow Jesus and go with us?

Quotes from Andrew Murray

"If we turn to His teaching, we find throughout that the obedience He rendered is the same He requires of everyone who would be His disciple." (16)

"Beware of a legal obedience: striving after a life of true obedience under a sense of duty." (91)

Questions for Reflection

1. Discuss Idleman's quote on the relationship of faith and following.
2. Discuss how Jesus fulfilled the Psalmist's expressions of obeying God with complete desire or all His heart. How do you stack up in comparison? In what way does the Gospel cover our shame for being so half-hearted?
3. Have you ever met anyone who literally engaged God like they were on a walk together? What was it like being with that person? What did you learn from Brother Lawrence?

4. Why is it wrong to allow sin to have a prominent place in your or other Christians' lives?
5. Try to capture in your own words why love matters most to God in all we do.

One-word command to Obey

"Go"

...Leave your gift there in front of the altar. First **go** and be reconciled to them; then come and offer your gift. (Matthew 5:24)

If anyone forces you to **go** one mile, **go** with them two miles. (Matthew 5:41)

But when you pray, **go** into your room, close the door and pray to your Father, who is unseen. as Then your Father, who sees what is done in secret, will reward you. (Matthew 6:6)

As you **go,** proclaim this message: 'The kingdom of heaven has come near.' (Matthew 10:7)

So **go** to the street corners and invite to the banquet anyone you find. (Matthew 22:9)

Therefore **go** and make disciples of all nations (Matthew 28:19a)

He said to her, "Daughter, you faith has healed you. **Go** in peace and be freed from your suffering." (Mark 5:34)

Jesus looked at him and loved him. "One thing you lack," he said, "**Go,** sell everything you have and give to the poor, and you will have treasure in heaven. Then come, follow me." (Mark 10:21)

He said to them, "**Go** into all the world and preach the gospel to all creation. (Mark 16:15)

Go! I am sending you out like lambs among wolves. (Luke 10:3)

"Then neither do I condemn you," Jesus declared. "**Go** now and leave your life of sin." (John 8:11)

"**Go,**" he told him, "wash in the Pool of Siloam" (this word means "sent"). So the man went and washing, and came home seeing. (John 9:7)

Then Thomas (also known as Didymus) said to the rest of the disciples, "Let us also **go,** that we may die with him." (John 11:16)

"Why do you call me, 'Lord, Lord,' and do not do what I say?" (Luke 6:46)

"As Jesus was saying these things, a woman in the crowd called out. 'Blessed is the mother who gave you birth and nursed you.' He replied, 'Blessed rather are those who hear the word of God and obey it.'" (Luke 11:27-28)

"More particularly, let us remember what the Lord Jesus Christ said in one of His lessons on mildness and forbearance.... May this precept, and these commands, strengthen our resolve to live in obedience to His sacred words, and in humility of mind."

(96AD- Bishop Clement of Rome, 1ˢᵗ letter to the Corinthians, ch13,).

"If a rabbi ultimately agreed to a would-be-disciple's request, and allowed him to become a disciple, the disciple-to-be agreed to totally submit to the rabbi's authority in all areas of interpreting the Scriptures for his life. This was a cultural given for all observant Jewish young men – something each truly wanted to do. As a result, each disciple came to a rabbinic relationship with a desire and a willingness to do just that - surrender to the authority of God's Word as interpreted by his Rabbi's view of Scripture.... Contrast total surrender to the authority of Jesus with a partial surrender, or an occasional surrender, a convenient surrender, or even token surrender to

Him. How would you assess your willingness factor in regards to surrendering all areas of your life to the authority of God's Word? When you do surrender, is it a willing surrender, or a surrender that arises from some form of resentful, obligatory obedience?"

(2007-Doug Greenwold,. Preserving Bible Times Reflection # 307)

Part Three

Obeying like the Apostles

Chapter Seven

The Apostles' Obedience - *Why It Matters*

Do you trust leadership today? By trust, I mean, the way we trust a chair we are about to sit down upon. We expect it to support us. To do its job. Not to collapse and leave us injured. So, do you really trust leaders today in that way? Probably not, in most areas of life.

New Testament era disciples, though, trusted their mentors, their rabbis. So much so, that they placed their lives in their hands, leaving the authority and safety of their own human fathers. David Bivin noted, "A special relationship developed between rabbi and disciple in which the rabbi became like a father.

In fact he was more than a father and was to be honored above the disciple's own father...."[53]

Disciples wanted to follow their leader. They intended to become just like their spiritual leaders. This was so well understood that Jesus summarized the normal rabbi-discipleship relationship with these words: **"A disciple is not above his teacher, but everyone who is perfectly trained will be like his teacher" (Luke 6:40-NKJV).**

Christians have no problem saying, "Jesus is the Head of the Church." Or, "I belong to Jesus." They would quickly affirm that, **'No one can lay any other foundation other than the one already laid, which is Jesus Christ"** (1 Corinthians 3:11). I believe that many Christians *say* these things but do not *live* them. Since Jesus is in heaven and no one is His deputy, policing the Church, it seems safe to say one thing and do another.

I am writing this chapter to dispel that myth. Jesus did leave His authorized representatives on earth, whose work involved building the Church and protecting us from both error and false teachers. They were called apostles and prophets. And, about them, Paul wrote, "**(You are) built on the foundation of the apostles and prophets, with Christ Jesus being**

the chief cornerstone" (Ephesians 2:20). You see, the Church did not say, "None of us are perfect. None of us are like Jesus. So, let's cut each other a break and not be too strict with how we live." That sounds like today. Paul sounded differently. He said the following:

> **"Follow my example as I follow the example of Christ."** (1 Corinthians 11:1)
>
> **"Did the word of God originate with you? Or are you the only people it has reached? If anybody thinks he is a prophet or spiritually gifted, let him acknowledge that what I am writing to you is the Lord's command."** (1 Corinthians 14:36-37)
>
> **"For you yourselves know how you ought to follow our example…. If anyone does not obey our instruction in this letter, take special note of him. Do not associate with him in order that he may feel ashamed. Yet do not regard him as an enemy, but warn him as a brother."** (2 Thessalonians 3:7,11)

You see, if Jesus commanded us to make disciples and if all disciples imitate their rabbi, then Jesus expects us to imitate His way of life. That means to obey Him and literally to follow Him. His pattern. His example. He molded the apostles into that pattern so that they could mold others. He made them effective "fishers of men." They were promised success. They would make disciples. Why are so few Christians actually imitating Jesus today? What pattern do we follow?

A Fear to Follow

Although democracy is often a wonderfully free way of life, New Testament times were not very democratic. Half of Rome's population of 1 million people were slaves. Those who lived in Palestine were largely not self-governed. They lived under Roman rule. Rebellions everywhere were severely crushed. Society was often governed very strictly by ever-changing laws. Citizens, employees, children were all expected to comply with the commands of their superiors—whether they be political leaders, employers or parents. The people of Palestine knew how to follow, even when they did not like it. Obedience and submission were not viewed as "necessary evils," but as the cornerstone of a community's stability.

We Americans generally have a hard time following, don't we? Freedom of thought, of word, of travel, define us. Great freedoms of expression and debate thrive here. Democracy, to us, often means freedom to protest and change. We have all seen how the spirit of doubting, questioning and even at times disregarding rules of our culture have been helpful. They can keep us and others from injustice and oppression.

But, sometimes dissent leads to a type of disobedience which gets us into trouble. Disagreements need to be resolved peacefully through discussion and debate. Civil disobedience has sometimes led to tremendous change and social progress. But not everything needs to be discussed and debated. In fact, real progress may be hindered when children, students, employees and citizens want to debate everything instead of simply doing what they have been told to do. Much trouble can be averted when we quickly yield and do what our superiors tell us to do. It appears to me that submission and obedience, law and order are shrinking in democratic America. In homes, churches, workplaces and neighborhoods there is a growing lack of trust, a growing readiness to rebel. A fear of following.

Was Jesus Undemocratic?

Does it surprise you that Jesus desires us to live a life of obedience and surrender? The following text, pivotal in its day, is often ignored in ours.

> **Jesus asked, "Suppose one of you has a servant plowing or looking after the sheep. Will he say to the servant when he comes in from the field, 'Come along now and sit down to eat'? Won't he rather say, 'Prepare my supper, get yourself ready and wait on me while I eat and drink; after that you may eat and drink'? Will he thank the servant because he did what he was told to do? So you also, when you have done everything you were told to do, should say, 'We are unworthy servants; we have only done our duty.'" (Luke 17:7-10)**

Jesus does not recommend that we follow our own thoughts, feelings and desires. In fact, as we will now see, Jesus commands us to follow Him and those whom He first discipled. Yes, Jesus wants us to follow the Apostles and the spiritual leaders whose lives imitate theirs.

If I asked you, what is the foundation of your faith? You would likely say, the Bible. But is it? My premise simply is that unless you are an obedient disciple of Jesus, you cannot really live biblically. That is because the New Testament clearly establishes a pattern or a lifestyle that all of us are to embrace. This way of life was patterned for the disciples by Jesus. And He then commanded them to teach others the same way of life that He had taught them to live. The model of Jesus allowed great freedom in many areas of life, so that true disciples did not all dress, eat, talk or work alike. But there were ever-present, trans-cultural elements of every believer's life that were non-negotiable. To disregard or discard these were to commit sin. And sinful patterns of life were never to be acceptable to His followers. Sin was not laughed-off in the New Testament Church, which was composed chiefly of disciples. It was normally dealt with as Jesus had clearly taught to deal with it.[54]

Free but Followers

I do not want to be misunderstood here. Jesus preached freedom **and** submission. Or better put, true freedom through faith in and submission to Him. His invitation to all potential disciples combined these two, **"Come to me, all you who are weary and burdened, and I will give you rest. Take my yoke upon you and learn from me, for I am gentle and humble in heart, and you will find rest for yours souls. For my yoke is easy and my burden is light" (Matthew 11:28-30).** There is a yoke, to be sure—but it is lighter than all others! And in a longer section, Jesus told those who had "believed him,"

"If you hold to my teaching (abide in my word-ESV), you are really my disciples. Then you will know the truth, and the truth will set you free." They answered him, "We are Abraham's descendants and have never been slaves of anyone. How can you say that we shall be set free?" Jesus replied, "I tell you the truth, everyone who sins is a slave to sin. Now a slave has no permanent

place in the family, but a son belongs to it forever. So if the Son sets you free, you will be free indeed" (John 8:31-36)

You see, only those who make His word their residence, who continue submitting their lives to what He has commanded and said, are true disciples. Only they are truly free. True disciples, alone, can be freed from the bondage of sin by the Son, who alone can free us. So, was Jesus undemocratic? Yes and no. Freedom was His goal. Obedience to Him and His Word was the way to reach that goal.

The concept of freedom to Jesus and the apostles was central to their teachings. Dr. Robert Banks termed "freedom in Christ," the "theological basis" of the writings of Paul. He wrote,

> "Paul uses the term *eleutheria* (freedom) or one of its cognates frequently throughout his writings, some twenty-nine times in all—only a little less often than *soteria* (salvation) or one of its allied terms."[55]

His chapter on "The Arrival of Radical Freedom," powerfully portrays how the gospel of Jesus leads to a freedom that absolutely amazed the Roman, Greek and Jewish cultures of the first century. **"It is for freedom that Christ has set us free. Stand firm, then, and do not let yourselves be burdened again by a yoke of slavery"** (Galatians 5:1).

The Chief Shepherd

Jesus is the Way. He is the Pattern, the Mold, the Map. When our lives do not follow His pattern, we are unshapely. Like a dress or a shirt that just doesn't hang or fit right. Something that we shouldn't waste our money on. When we do not reflect His image, we are like a coin minted from a counterfeit cast. A hoax that can't buy anything. Of no real benefit except to make noise in our pockets. Whenever we walk a path not pleasing to Him, we get lost. And we lead others astray. Peter called Jesus, **"the Chief Shepherd"** (1 Peter 5:4). Just as sheep follow their shepherd, the apostles followed Jesus. Jesus is the Head Shepherd. The Trainer and Model of all other spiritual shepherds. He is the Guide of our guides. That is why pastors are sometimes called "under-shepherds" We are all supposed to be submissive or obedient to Jesus.

Shepherds are not very democratic. They know what is best and strategize accordingly. We all want the Great Shepherd Psalm (23) to be read at our funerals. You know, **"The Lord is my Shepherd…."** Whether or not we choose to live, to walk and talk, with the Lord as our Shepherd, we feel as though every Christian has a right to that psalm. Even if we rarely thought about Jesus or spoke in His name. The fact not to forget is that Jesus spoke about all His sheep. He said, **"My sheep listen to my voice. And I know them. And they follow me. I give to them eternal life, and they shall never perish. ; no one can snatch them out of my hand"** (John 10:27-28). We like to stress what passages say about us. Consider also what that passage says about Jesus. He speaks. We listen. He knows each one intimately. We are known, related to, beloved. He leads. We follow. He gives them eternal life. We receive life now and forever from Him, alone. No one can take His sheep from His personal care. We are safe when the Lord is our Shepherd.

The Path that the Shepherd Chooses

Peter spoke of Jesus' example in this way, **"If you suffer for doing good and you endure it, this is commendable before God. <u>To this you were called</u>, because Christ suffered for you, leaving you an example, that <u>you should follow in his steps</u>"** (1 Peter 2:20b-21). Jesus has left us all with an example to follow. He is the Way. We are to follow Him, even in His life of suffering. The night He relentlessly taught them that His command was LOVE, He also said, **"Remember the words I spoke to you, 'No servant is greater than his master.' If they persecuted me, they will persecute you also. If they obeyed my teaching, they will obey yours also. They will treat you this way because of my name, for they do not know the One who sent me"** (John 15:20-21). Did you see that? To Jesus, persecution and obedience to Him are connected. If they persecuted…if they obeyed. True Christians are the objects of both the persecution and lack of obedience. The world persecutes and does not obey disciples.

So, fast forward to today. When we take away the demand to obey, we take away the need to be persecuted. No obedience = no persecution. The renowned martyr Ignatius, Bishop of Antioch was on his way to Rome to be killed for his faith at the end of the first Century. Listen carefully to what he wrote to Christian churches as he passed through their cities, and wonder, would we ever read such words in America today?

> "As I go about in these chains … I sing songs of praise to the churches; and I pray for their corporate as well as their spiritual unity—for both of these are the gifts of Jesus Christ, our never-failing Life. May they be one in their faith, and in their love, which transcends all other virtues; but chiefest of all may they be one with Jesus and the Father, since <u>it is only by enduring in Him all the prince of the world's indignities</u>, yet still eluding his clutches, that we can come to the presence of God….
>
> "<u>There are two different coinages, so to speak, in circulation, God's and the world's, each with its own distinctive marking. Unbelievers carry the stamp of the world; while the faithful in love bear the stamp of God the Father,</u>

through Jesus Christ. Unless we are ready to die in conformity with His Passion (Death), His life is not in us.... "Farewell. See that there is a godly unity among you, and a spirit that is above all divisions; for this is Jesus Christ." (Ignatius to the Magnesians, chapters 1, 5 & 15).

Disciples obey. That is why they suffer. Even today.

Follow Me

Paul discipled the Corinthians quite clearly, so he wrote, **"Follow my example as I follow the example of Christ"** (1 Corinthians 11:1). He was greatly upset when anyone was placed before Christ as a model. Even when he, himself was followed at the expense of Jesus! He strongly scolded the Corinthians,

> **"Brothers and sisters, I could not address you as people who live by the Spirit but as people who are still worldly—mere infants in Christ. I gave you milk, not solid food, for you were not yet ready for it. Indeed,**

you are still not ready. You are still worldly. For since there is jealousy and quarreling among you, are you not worldly? Are you not acting like mere humans? For when one says, "I follow Paul," and another, "I follow Apollos," are you not mere human beings? What, after all, is Apollos? And what is Paul? Only servants, through whom you came to believe—as the Lord has assigned to each his task. I planted the seed, Apollos watered it, but God has been making it grow. So neither the one who plants nor the one who waters is anything, but only God, who makes things grow. The one who plants and the one who waters have one purpose, and they will each be rewarded according to their own labor. For we are co-workers in God's service; you are God's field, God's building. By the grace God has given me, I laid a foundation as a wise builder, and someone else is building on it. But each one should build with care. For no one can lay any foundation other

than the one already laid, which is Jesus Christ. (1 Cor 3:1-11)

He then wrote, **"I urge you to imitate me."** (1 Corinthians 4:16). He had given them a pattern to follow. And he expected them to follow it. He did this everywhere and to everyone because he was making disciples of Jesus. He was following Christ's pattern and requiring others to be similarly patterned.

So, to the Philippians he wrote, **"Join with others in following my example, brothers, and take note of those who live accordingly to the pattern we gave you"** (Philippians 3:17). And, later, **"Whatever you have learned or received or heard from me, or seen in me—put it into practice. And the God of peace will be with you"** (Philippians 4:9). And to two of his own disciples, Timothy and Titus, he very clearly reminded them of the Christ-pattern passed on to them which they were to impress upon the lives of others:

"If you point these things out to the brothers and sisters, you will be a good minister of Christ Jesus, brought up in the truths of the faith

and of the good teaching that you have followed." (1 Timothy 4:6)

"Don't let anyone look down on you because you are young, but set an example for believers in speech, in life, in love, in faith, and in purity." (1 Timothy 4:12)

"These are the things you are to teach and insist on. If anyone teaches false doctrines and does not agree to the sound instruction of our Lord Jesus Christ and to godly teaching, he is conceited and understands nothing." (1 Timothy 6:2-3)

Timothy, guard what has been entrusted to your care." (1 Timothy 6:20)

"What you have heard from me, keep as the pattern of sound teaching, with faith and love in Christ Jesus." (2 Timothy 1:6)

"You then, my son, be strong in the grace that is in Christ Jesus. And

the things you have heard me say, in the presence of many witnesses entrust to reliable men who will also be qualified to teach others." (2 Timothy 2:1-2)

"You, however, know all about my teaching, my way of life, my purpose, faith, patience, love, endurance, persecutions, sufferings... In fact, everyone who wants to live a godly life in Christ Jesus will be persecuted, while evil men and imposters go from bad to worse, deceiving and being deceived. But as for you, continue in what you have learned and have become convinced of...." (2 Timothy 3:10-14)

"You must teach what is in accord with sound doctrine... In everything set them an example by doing what is good... These are the things you should teach. Encourage and rebuke with all authority. Do not let anyone despise you. " (Titus 2:1, 7, 15)

In portraying Luke's intent in writing his Gospel and Acts, Richard Longenecker summarized,

> "...It is quite true that Luke's major interest in the writing of his two volumes seems to have been the everyday matter of Christian discipleship—that is, setting out for his readers ... the manner in which one should live as a follower of Jesus." And earlier, " For Luke, the church is only faithful to its calling as it perseveres in the teaching and the tradition of the apostles, who constitute the human link with Jesus. And Christian discipleship is only authentic as it does likewise."[56]

So, respected Evangelical scholarship establishes discipleship as the goal of Luke's writing and challenges us today with questioning if present-day discipleship patterns actually follow the apostolic mode which was linked with Jesus. Much, sadly, is lost when there is little parallel between our methods and that of the apostles, who followed Jesus.

Following the Disciples who were trained by the Apostles

When Paul left the Ephesian elders, he knew that his discipleship would be the focus of demonic attack. So he solemnly warned them, **"Keep watch over yourselves and all the flock over which the Lord has made you overseers. Be shepherds of the church of God, which he bought with his own blood. I know that after I leave, savage wolves will come in among you and will not spare the flock. Even from your own number men will arise and distort the truth in order to draw away disciples after them. So be on your guard! Remember that for three years I never stopped warning each of you night and day with tears."** (Acts 20:28-31).

Ever since Jesus commanded, **"Make disciples,"** the devil has tried to corrupt the process of discipleship. Jesus chose and sent authorized representatives, apostles, into the world to initiate that work. So, their teaching and lifestyle have been received and followed by the faithful down through the centuries. In the second generation of the early church, it was common to hear words like these:

"This salvation, which was first announced by the Lord, was confirmed to us by those who heard him. God also testified to it by signs, wonders and various miracles, and gifts of the Holy Spirit distributed according to his will." (Hebrews 2:3-4)

"Remember your leaders, who spoke the word of God to you. Consider the outcome of their way of life and imitate their faith. Jesus Christ is the same yesterday andtoday and forever." (Hebrews 13:7-8)

"Obey your leaders and submit to their authority. They keep watch over you as men who must give an account. Obey them so that their work will be a joy, not a burden...." (Hebrews 13:17)

Even early, non-biblical sources, like the Didache, reminded 1st-century believers to follow their leaders as they followed Jesus. "See that you do not neglect the commandments of the Lord, but keep them just as you received them, without any additions or subtractions of your own" (The Didache, 1:4).

Renewal, Revival & Reformation

The reason it matters that we know and follow the apostolic model is that the Bible commands us to do so. Jesus formed them and they formed the Church after them in the exact pattern of life Jesus had used. All through the ages, Christians have cried out for Jesus to help them when the Church had sunk to a low stage. Words like, "Renew us!" "Revive us!" "Send a Reformation!" have echoed throughout World Christian history. And whenever God answered, what happened? A renewal of biblical discipleship happened! People cut through the tradition, the baggage and discovered Jesus again by the power of the Holy Spirit.

Did you catch the similarity in all of those words? They are "re" words, all beginning with the same prefix. "Re" signifies going back and returning or regaining something that existed before. The "new wine" and "new wine skins" that must be **re**newed is biblical discipleship. The new life (vivification) that is

revived is "walking with God." The new form that replaces the traditions of church practice, bringing **re**formation, is the age-old pattern passed on by Jesus to His first disciples and, by them and others, to succeeding generations.

The Holy Spirit can take us back into a life of following Jesus today. The New Testament epistles describe that life of discipleship as being "**in Christ**." But the form or pattern of that life will look like the apostles way of life. By this standard of discipleship, we are commanded to **"Test everything. Hold on to the good. Avoid every kind of evil"** (1 Thessalonians 5:21-22). The apostle John, remembering the testing of some in the church wrote, "**They went out from us, but they did not really belong to us. For if they had belonged to us, they would have remained with us; but their going showed that none of them belonged to us**" (1 John 2:19).

Do we belong to the apostolic tradition? Have we heard the call of Jesus and obeyed Him, as they did? And as they taught? Do we want to be seen as a true heir of the Early Church in Acts? Then let us live and obey as they did, for of them it was written,

"They devoted themselves to the apostles teaching and to the fellowship, to the breaking of bread and to prayer. Everyone was filled with awe, and many wonders and miraculous signs were done by the apostles. All the believers were together and had everything in common. Selling their possessions and goods, they gave to anyone as he had need. Every day they continued to meet together with glad and sincere hearts, praising God and enjoying the favor of all the people. And the Lord (Jesus) added to their number daily those who were being saved." (Acts 2:42-47).

The next chapter will truly surprise you as we now turn to obeying Jesus as the apostles obeyed Him.

A 21st Century Disciple's Story

My name is Mike. When Jesus renewed my call to follow Him the hardest obedience He demanded came in the form of *total surrender*. He demanded that I follow Him into places and situations that were uncomfortable.

At the time of my renewal to follow Jesus I was on the very edge of giving up my pastorate and looking for a much more comfortable and inviting community at which to serve.

You see, God had called me into an urban community suffering from drug abuse, prostitution, alcoholism and unstable families. He called me to a small church with little finances and sparse attendance. After ministering in that community for the last 8 years, the people's rejection of the gospel became too much too bear. We opened a free Christian school and the community refused to take advantage of it. We gave away food, clothing and anything our limited budget would afford, but still there was an outright rejection of the gospel. Many months my wife and I neglected our personal bills to ensure that the utilities were not turned off. Those that did come were from outside the community and their attendance was sporadic at best.

Depression began to set in and the closing of the church doors became a reality. I started thinking more and more of how to shut down the church and where I would move to. My hope was lost and it became increasingly difficult to hide it from the congregation. This loss of hope revealed itself in the form of anger towards the congregation. Our frustration grew and many Sundays I did all I could, just to show up for the worship service.

Just at the point of giving up I received a renewed call to follow Jesus. I learned what the Bible meant about being a disciple. I knew that I first had to become a disciple before I could disciple others. Through my discipleship training and praying with others I began to see that following Jesus calls for total surrender. I had to be willing to give up my own comfortability and follow Jesus into the community that He has chosen for me.

Since my renewed call and obeying Jesus, my prayer life has totally changed! Prayer was not a priority in my life or the life of our congregation. Through prayer, God led us to go on a 30-day fast of just fruits, veggies and water. It was during this time we really cried out to God for the community and others.

This resulted in having four teams do a prayer walk through the community, praying specifically that God would touch the hearts of the people that live on the same block as the church. The very next Sunday 6 individuals from the same block came in for the worship service. You might think that small, but it was BIG for us.

Obeying Jesus has now become central to my preaching, teaching and our congregational life. People expect to do something every week in response to the Word!

Another result of obeying Jesus is being connected to other disciples in the city who consistently lift our prayers and concerns before the Lord. It's a wonderful feeling to know you are not walking alone. We still have a long way to go, but we are certain and ready to follow Jesus where He is—and He is in this difficult community. Thinking of closing the doors is no longer in our minds. We now know that God will provide all that we need as long as we follow His Son. The congregation has an air of excitement as we pray. We now understand that you cannot follow Jesus without obeying Jesus. Come and follow Jesus with us.

Quotes from Andrew Murray

"Christ wants us from the very entrance to His school to vow complete obedience…. Wholehearted obedience is not the end but the beginning of our school life." (82)

"In Matthew 28:19-20, Christ does not teach or argue, ask or plead; He simply commands. He has trained His disciples in obedience...How miserably the church has failed in obeying the command!" (96-97)

Questions for Reflection

1. How deeply do you trust your church leadership? Enough to watch and follow their example?
2. Did the discussion on democracy bother you at all? If so, why?
3. What did you think about the difference between the way a Christian and the disciple would look at Psalm 23?
4. How do you think the message of submission and obedience to others in the Church would be received by your friends? By the Church's youth?
5. When you have prayed for renewal and revival, did you really grasp WHAT you were wanting to be renewed and revived? What pattern or reality were you hoping to return to?

One-word command to Obey

"Obey"

If you want to enter into life, **obey** the commandments (Matthew 19:17)

So you must **obey** them and **do** everything they tell you. But do not do what they do, for they do not practice what they preach (Matthew 23:3)

Blessed rather are those who hear the word of God and **obey** it. (Luke 11:28)

If you love me, you will **obey** what I command. (John 14:15)

We must **obey** God rather than men! (Acts 5:29)

But thanks be to God that, though you used to be slaves to sin, you wholeheartedly **obeyed** the form of teaching to which you were entrusted. (Romans 6:17)

He will punish those who do not know God and do not **obey** the gospel of our Lord Jesus. (2 Thessalonians 1:8)

Those who **obey** his commands live in him, and he in them. (1 John 3:24)

"Submit"

Everyone must **submit** himself to the governing authorities, for there is no authority except that which God has established. The authorities that exist have been established by God. (Romans 13:1)

Submit to one another out of reverence for Christ. (Ephesians 5:21)

Submit yourselves then to God. (James 4:7)

How much more should we **submit** to the Father of our spirits and live! (Hebrews 12:9)

Obey your (spiritual) leaders and **submit** to their authority. (Hebrews 13:17)

"Jesus went up on a mountainside and called to him those he wanted, and they came to him. He appointed twelve that they might be with him and that he might send them out to preach and to have authority to drive out demons. These are the twelve he appointed: Simon (to whom he gave the name Peter), James son of Zebedee and his brother John (to them he gave the name Boanerges, which means "sons of thunder"), Andrew, Philip, Bartholomew, Matthew, Thomas, James son of Alphaeus, Thaddaeus, Simon the Zealot and Judas Iscariot, who betrayed him." (Mark 3:13-19)

"You did not choose me, but I chose you and appointed you so that you might go and bear fruit—fruit that will last—and so that whatever you ask in my name the Father will give you." (John 15:16)

"At the time of their call they were exceedingly ignorant, narrow-minded, superstitious, full of Jewish prejudices, misconceptions, and animosities. They had much to unlearn of what was bad, as well as much to learn of what was good, and they were slow both to learn and to unlearn."

"The Twelve, at the period of their first trial mission, were not fit to preach the gospel, or to do good works, either among Samaritans or Gentiles. Their hearts were too narrow, their prejudices too strong; there was too much of the Jew and too little of the Christian, in their character."

(Prof. AB Bruce, The Training of the Twelve, pp 14, 101)

Chapter Eight

The Apostles' Obedience - *With Flaws Exposed*

A general survey of the New Testament reveals the foundational and essential part that the chosen, prepared and commissioned apostles of Jesus played in the planting, growing and multiplying of the Church of the first century. What kind of men were they? They were deemed, "**unschooled, ordinary men**,"(Acts 4:13) by the Sanhedrin because they were, well, not educated in the way the official leaders were educated. And they did not come from the pedigree of most Jewish leaders, either. Nevertheless, those men were uniquely chosen and trained by the Incarnate Son of God, to prove several points. Paul made some of those reasons clear to the Corinthians, when he wrote that,

> **"Not many of you were wise by human standards; not many were influential;not many of noble birth. But God chose the foolish things of the world to shame thewise; ...the weak things of the world to shame the strong; ... the lowly things of this world—and the things that are not—to nullify the things that are, so that no one may boast before him.... Therefore, as it is written, 'Let him who boasts boast in the Lord"** (1 Corinthians 1:26-31).

New Testament era servants of God were, largely, unschooled, poor, unimpressive and easily overlooked. Why? The text gives the following strategic purposes: (1) To challenge and embarrass the well-educated. (2) To expose the moral, spiritual and social weaknesses of the highly-placed in Roman society. (3) To eradicate the system of honor among humans, so that they were left without any reason to brag. (4) And all of this to prove ONE GREAT POINT—no one ever achieves anything except by the will and mercy of God.

To prove that what is impossible with us is not only possible, but likely, with God!

So, as you read this chapter, forget the high and heroic thoughts you had of these first true Christians. And think highly of Jesus, alone. We must realize that none of them, at their best, wanted anyone exalted except Jesus. They would want YOU to receive from them ONLY what they had received from Him. We honor them all for all they BECAME. But all that they became was by His grace. And YOU ALL can become amazing trophies of grace, too—if you will dare to lay aside your honor, your strength and your glory—and give them all to Jesus!

They were not Spiritual Standouts

When apologists list the evidences for the Bible's divine inspiration, there is one that is never left out. An argument that often makes critics scratch their heads. The Bible's human writers revealed their own major flaws. The heroes and heroines described throughout its sacred pages are clearly presented as sinners in need of a Savior. Who, writing on their own impetus, would reveal their deepest, secret iniquities? Why parade your own shame for the ages when you could make your point otherwise? No one would do so unless they had to. Unless they were writing under the control of another who demanded it. The Other, the Controller, was the Holy Spirit of God, who wanted it to be clear, that from Adam to the Apostle John, **"there is none righteous, not even one**." The only true hero in the Bible is the Lord Jesus Christ!

Following the amazing conversion of Matthew the tax collector, the Pharisees asked the disciples, **"Why does your teacher eat with tax collectors and sinners?" (Matthew 9:11)**. Notice that Matthew, when writing his own Gospel account, noted that he, himself, was a social stigma. A wretch so corrupt that the leaders' question left the disciples speechless. His inclusion to their group was, indeed, even an embarrassment to them. Matthew continues the story beyond their silence, **"On hearing this, Jesus said, It is not the healthy who need a doctor, but the sick… For I have not come to call the righteous, but sinners"** (Matthew 9:12-13).

Come, Ye Sinners

The apostles were not forced upon Jesus. He did not desperately choose the Twelve out of a small sampling. Vast multitudes followed Him. Thousands upon thousands are pictured in the Gospels as being so enamored with Him that they would dangerously imperil themselves just to hear Him and watch His amazing actions. They did not want to miss a thing. On one late afternoon occasion, when surrounded by 4,000 men, plus women and children, Jesus said, **"I have compassion for these people; they have already been with me three days and have nothing to eat. If I send them home hungry, they will collapse on the way, because some of them have come a long distance"** (Mark 8:2-3). Thousands would risk their own health and safety just to be near Him. Indeed, Jesus had many to choose from.

But Jesus did not choose disciples like other rabbis did. Karen Kogler helps us understand,

"How did becoming a disciple of Jesus compare to becoming a disciple of other first century groups? Like Greek learning groups that followed Socrates, and like groups that developed on this model (scribes, Pharisees and Essenes), the basis was a personal relationship with the master and a commitment to be with him and learn from him. It was not primarily a commitment to knowledge or beliefs. It included a lifelong commitment to his cause.

"Jesus called individuals to be his disciple. Although they had the freedom to reject the call, the choice to become a disciple was not entirely their own, as it was in other groups. Jesus made that plain when he told his disciples,

"You did not choose me but I chose you." you." (John 15:16). A man who wanted to be a scribe would select a master under whom he wanted to study; he would then be either accepted or rejected by the master. Becoming a Pharisee, Sadducee or Essene was a matter of accepting the teachings and way of life of the group. Becoming a priest was limited to men of certain families, but the individuals in those families likely had some choice as to whether or not to serve as priests. Jesus' call was powerful. The power and authority in Jesus himself, and the impact of his call, is shown in that all four Gospel writers, early in their narrative of Jesus' ministry, include stories of that call and of the way it changed the lives of those who were called. The response is immediate and total.

"Jesus extended his call to an unusual assortment of people. Unlike priests, there was no requirement of racial purity. Unlike the Pharisees, he did not fellowship only with ritually pure people. Unlike the Sadducees, he did not favor a certain social class. It is likely that the call of Matthew (Matthew 9:9-13) is included in the Gospels not simply to show how Matthew became one of the Twelve, but to show that Jesus called a tax collector in the same way and with the same response as he called Peter, Andrew, James and John, and to show the negative response of the Pharisees and scribes to Jesus' association, and feasting, with sinners.

Women are specifically mentioned as following him, while they are virtually unmentioned in contemporary sources describing other groups. Jesus' group of disciples spent a great deal of time together, and their adjustment to each other must have been interesting and challenging at times."[57]

Mark 3:13 describes Jesus' method of selection in this way, **"Jesus...called to him those he wanted."** They are not noted as being the smartest, the strongest, the wealthiest or the most handsome. Yet they were chosen. He had His reasons. But, as we shall soon see, when given the opportunity to describe themselves, the apostles did not think much of themselves. And neither did others. Jesus chose weak, selfish sinners and made them into His disciples. They were not supermen. Just men. The hymnist captures His call well in the famous hymn,

"Come, ye sinners, poor and wretched,
weak and wounded, sick and sore;
Jesus ready stands to save you, full of
pity joined with power:

He is able, he is able, he is able, he is willing; doubt no more.
Come, ye weary, heavy laden, bruised and broken by the fall;
If you tarry till you're better, you will never come at all:
Not the righteous, not the righteous, not the righteous,
Sinners Jesus came to call."[58]

Don't Miss the Point

If discipleship was central to Jesus' life, it ought to be to ours, too. New Testament scholar Richard Longenecker saw many writers making too little of discipleship, missing the point about its simple power in driving Christ's first followers. He sensed that the subject of discipleship "needs better biblical rootage than it usually receives in the popular press and better personal application than it usually receives in scholarly writings." So, he made it the first chosen subject of the McMaster New Testament Studies Series, which he edited. This excellent series, begun in 1996, was "designed to address particular themes in the New Testament that are (or should be) of crucial concern to Christians today."⁵⁹ That our theme of discipleship should be granted **first place** in the series shows that these scholars are convinced that New Testament discipleship is "a subject that lies at the heart of all Christian thought, life, and ministry."⁶⁰

In the first volume of the series, "Patterns of Discipleship in the New Testament," Mark Hurtado, a New Testament Professor in Scotland, made the point that "Mark's story of Jesus is vitally concerned with discipleship."⁶¹ And, unlike the other Gospels, which have some dealings with the birth of Jesus, "Mark begins with Jesus' baptism because baptism is where the life of discipleship begins."⁶²

Prof. Hurtado reveals the amazing ways that Mark portrayed the twelve apostles in his account of Jesus and His discipleship. And it is by these amazing facts that we will explore the nature of the apostles' obedience, since we are to follow Jesus as they did. It is far too often our human tendency to unduly exalt our favorites and ignore their flaws.

Here is the staggering truth revealed by Hurtado's research and writing: "Nearly every scholarly analysis recognizes the negative ways in which the Twelve are treated in Mark's Gospel."[63] Mark views the apostles in a more critical light than do the other Gospel writers. The thought initially surprises us—Mark's portrayal of the Twelve highlights their flaws and weaknesses more than their virtues and strengths! Why would he do that? Or better, why would the Spirit inspire him to write in such a negative way?

The point not to be missed is the very one with which Jesus taught His disciples to conclude their prayers: **"thine is the glory, forever. Amen!"** Yes, it is remarkable that the Twelve left everything to follow Jesus. But they did not leave their pride, ambition and prejudice. At the end they all "deserted him and fled," (Mark 14:50), and only Jesus stays standing. To Him be all praise, honor and glory. I trust that you will be encouraged with the reality of His faithfulness and forgiveness as we look briefly at the apostolic failures, knowing that we will follow no better than they did.

Fumbling but Fruitful Disciples

Though Mark begins with a favorable account of their first days with Jesus, it is not soon after that the apostles' halos begin to fade. Mark subtly introduces us to the inevitable difficulties of discipleship in 3:19, when listing the Twelve for the first time, he wrote, **"and Judas Iscariot, who betrayed him."** It is here, with the first mention of this truly amazing and honored group, that the reality of their imperfection is revealed. We have a tendency to create unrealistic expectations by giving only one-sided representations of our spiritual heroes. The Holy Spirit did not want Mark to do that and probably does not want us to do so either.

Ten Texts that Warn all Disciples

I am indebted to Hurtado for unveiling how Mark told the amazing story of Jesus by simultaneously accounting His disciples' difficulties.[64] It often takes a biblical expert to point such things out because they could be easily glossed over by those of us who are more casual readers. I will list the main texts, highlight the blunders and make some practical remarks that I hope will both warn and encourage the reader. It would serve you well to open your Bibles and read Mark's texts before reading my remarks. Mark wants us to realize just how bad disciples can be, so that we will never take our eyes off of the One we are always ultimately to be following - Jesus!

1. Mark 3:13-19 (The Choosing of the Twelve)

Judas was called "a thief" by John (John 12:6), and one who did not really care for the poor. He was a complex man who struggled with greed, cowardice and ultimately, betrayal. Someone with whom money mattered a lot. But Mark will be fair and show that, even in the context of John's statement (the anointing of Jesus' head at Bethany at the beginning of the last week of His life), there were other apostles who agreed with Judas' assessment that Jesus had "**wasted**" the perfume that should have been sold (Mark 14:4-5) and used more beneficially. Judas saw the miracles, helped distribute the loaves to the 5000, went out on missions, cast out demons, preached the gospel. And ended up in hell. The vices were not unique to Judas, even as they are not characteristic only of apostates today. Their deadly seeds are sown in us all. Follow Jesus.

2. Mark 4:10-13 (The Parable of the Sower)

The Twelve were given "**the secret of the kingdom of God**," (v.11) but, Mark notes, they had a hard time understanding it. Sometimes, we aren't as sharp as we should be. At times, through pride or fear, we do not ask questions that we should. Even we who are disciples and not "**outsiders**" can be extremely dull. We all need help. The Illuminator, the Spirit must help us. There is much that can be discerned only with His help (1 Corinthians 2:14). We should all seek to be filled with the Holy Spirit.

3. Mark 4:35-41 (Jesus Awakes and Calms the Storm)

Not only do we disciples struggle with our understanding, being filled at times with confusion. We fight with fear and doubt. Even during a miracle! Jesus asked them, **"Why are you so afraid?"** (v. 40.) Not a bad question to ask yourself and others at times. Jesus really helps us by the follow-up question, **"Do you**

still have no faith?" (v. 40.) In that second question, we have a clue as to how fears can dominate disciples. Faithlessness precedes fear. Or put another way, doubts feed fears. What we are inside is significant. Emotions are not neutral. They matter to Jesus. It is possible to see miracles, as the apostles had seen, and not have one's faith grow significantly. Praise is the response of faith. Prayer is the response of faith. People without prayer and praise are **wasting** God's daily providences of grace in their lives. They are like the crowds who beheld Jesus' miracles and heard His teachings, but did not believe. Don't be a disciple who coasts through even a day. Believe. Praise Him. Pray.

4. Mark 6:45-52 (Jesus Walks on the Water)

In the second sea miracle, the apostles do even worse than in the first! They are terrified. They are screaming in fear. But that is not the big issue. When He climbed into the boat, **"they were completely amazed, for they had not understood about the loaves; their hearts were hardened"** (vv. 51-52). Mark does not brighten the story as Matthew does, by telling of Peter's walking on the water.

Somehow, the apostles missed the message of the miracle of the 5000 being fed. They were there and busy and missed it. Don't miss or underestimate what God is doing around you! But the problem is deeper than that in these disciples. Mark exposes the sin of their hearts. They were growing hard. In fact, it is the passive voice, their hearts were hardened, a discipline imposed by God. He had earlier warned them, **"Consider carefully what you hear. With the measure you use it will be measured to you—and even more. Whoever has will be given more; whoever does not have, even what he has will be taken from him"** (Mark 4:24-25). Disciples are accountable for what they see and hear. Nothing is to be wasted. It is all to be gathered up and used for the advancement of the Kingdom. Jesus' popularity is growing and the disciples' hearts are hardening. Beware of success. Use for God and others what you have and more will be given to you. Keep your hearts soft. Be filled with compassion and generosity.

5. Mark 8:14-21 (The Leaven or Yeast of the Pharisees)

Now their problem of priorities is confronted. The disciples' hearts, like ours, keep growing harder when there is no true repentance. We do not read of or see repentance in the Mark's texts, so they get more confused about what Jesus is saying. What He is emphasizing. The Pharisees and Herod focused on the outward over inward or the physical over the spiritual. They did so because they could not see what mattered most. Jesus was now asking His disciples if they understood how irrelevant the physical realm was. Physical bread? The Creator is upset because they forgot bread? Please! What matters most to you, the outward or the inward? The car, the dress, the promotion, the house, the money, the looks? Paul understood and said, **"For the kingdom of God is not a matter of eating and drinking. But righteousness, peace and joy in the Holy Spirit"** (Romans 14:17). Open your eyes and see. Open your ears and hear. Listen to Jesus and respond!

6. Mark 8:31-33 (Jesus Predicts His Death and Rebukes Peter)

Just when you think you have it all, whoosh – away it goes. Peter confesses that

Jesus is the Messiah. This is where Matthew reveals Jesus' praise of Peter, the rock. Mark knows how hard the discipleship road is to walk and wants to warn all his readers that even the greatest can fall. Even the revelator can become the mouthpiece of Satan! And immediately so. The negative response is significant by Jesus in His calling Peter, "Satan!" In saying that Peter's mind was consumed by "the things of men" (v33). Disciples beware! Or as Paul would later warn, **"So, if you think you are standing firm, be careful that you don't fall!"** (1 Corinthians 10:12). Clothe yourselves with humility. Everything you have is a gift from God's grace. Learn from Peter to think, no to PRAY, before you speak. And to follow Jesus in bearing your cross. Much good came through His suffering and will come through yours as you follow Him!

7. Mark 9:2-8 (The Transfiguration of Jesus)

This is an amazing story. Jesus is transformed before their eyes. God the Father speaks from heaven. In the greatest light, Mark shows the apostles walking in darkness. When Peter speaks, he misspeaks because **"they were so frightened"** (v.6). Again, they were confused, not understanding **"what rising from the dead meant."** (v. 10). The more glorious the experience, the more confused they get. Experiences assure us of nothing, if we do not believe what we see and do what we hear. If Jesus is eclipsed by anyone or anything, even by Moses and Elijah. Make room for Jesus. Listen to Jesus. **"Now that you know these things, you will be blessed if you do them"** (John 13:17). Disciples obey.

8. Mark 9:14-29 (The Healing of the Demonized Boy)

Now the reversal is almost complete. The weakness of the disciples is manifested at a new level. When they had known and seen little, they had been supernaturally used by God. **"They drove out many demons, and anointed many sick people with oil and healed them"** (Mark 6:13). Now a man tells Jesus, **"I asked your disciples to drive out the spirit, but they could not"** (v. 18). Jesus is angered. He calls His disciples **"O unbelieving generation"** and groans, **"How long shall I stay with you? How long shall I put up with you?"** (v.19). He heals the boy and the disciples wonder why they could not.

Jesus taught them, **"This kind can come out only by prayer"** (v. 29). Disciples can anger and exasperate Love Incarnate! But, **"Love is patient. Love is kind."** (1 Cor 13:4.) He graciously answers when they come, confused to Him. Pray without ceasing. Do not presume on God based on past success. Prayer is the position of weakness, of humility. **"Humble yourselves before the Lord and he will lift you up"** (James 4:10).

9. Mark 14:10-72 (The Upper Room, Gethsemane & Arrest of Jesus)

As flagrant as some of the disciples' digressions have been, we now reach the zenith in the passion narratives of Mark 14-15. Jesus predicts their fall and restoration. But Peter **"and all the rest" declare, "even if I have to die with you, I will never disown you."** (14:31). You know the story. You know who was right and who was weak. All of them run away in fear. Mark, himself, flees naked out of the garden (14:51-52). Maybe that is why he is so relentless in his Gospel about warning disciples of their weakness and of Christ's strength. He would later be a good colleague of Peter, who, even though the greatest disciple, utterly disowned Jesus. Three times, even with a cursing oath (14:71). Deeper than this no disciple can go. Despair. Depression. Anger. Resentment. Fear. Hopelessness. You name it. You have likely NEVER been there. That low. Mark knows. He wants you to feel it. Because something unbelievable is about to happen. But not quite yet.

10. Mark 16:7-14

The negative focus of Mark is almost over. But, he so wants his readers to trust only Christ, to never trust in their flesh, to never walk away from faith—that he paints the picture even bleaker. Christ has risen! But the apostles are nowhere to be found. The female disciples are all we see. They are out even if they aren't quite sure why. And God blesses them. Their faith, their love, their duty. **"Go tell his disciples and Peter, He is going ahead of you into Galilee. There you will see him, just as he told you"** (16:7). Peter is no longer listed as among the disciples. He will have to be restored. His public renunciation will demand a public confession and repentance (John 21). But watch the women. Disciples obey! How do they respond to the angel? **"Trembling** and bewildered, the women went out and fled from the tomb. They said nothing to anyone, because they were afraid."** (Mark 16:8). Earlier Jesus had sent out 72 and told them, **"Go! I am sending you out like lambs among wolves... Do not greet anyone on the road"** (Luke 10:3-4). That is what these women did. God's messenger told them who to go to and what to say. That is precisely what they did! Why? Disciples obey!

When they arrived with their witness, **"they did not believe it."** (16:11). After Jesus appeared to the two walking on the Road to Emmaus, they returned and reported to the Twelve, **"but they did not believe them either."** (16:13). Has Mark's real but negative reporting on the apostles throughout his Gospel convinced you of the difficulty and promise of discipleship? These abject failures were transformed by the power of the Holy Spirit into selfless, loving world changers. But before they were changed, Jesus had something else to tell them.

"Later Jesus appeared to the Eleven as they were eating; he rebuked them for their lack of faith and their

stubborn refusal to believe those who had seen him after he had risen. He said to them, Go into all the world and preach the good news to all creation. Whoever believes and is baptized will be saved, but whoever does not believe will be condemned" (Mark 16:14-16).

Hurtado concludes,

"Mark's story about Jesus is vitally concerned with discipleship. There is ample sayings…in which Jesus instructs and inspires the Twelve and subsequent disciples. Jesus' disciples, especially the Twelve, are memorably presented in a complex role as … demonstrating the difficulties and failures to which disciples are subject.

"Mark also boldly and dramatically counterposes the shortcomings and failures of the Twelve to Jesus' exemplary behavior in order to portray the demands of discipleship, with Jesus himself as the object and example of discipleship. Jesus' authoritative promise of restoration ofthe Twelve to fellowship after their shameful collapse makes Jesus' calling the sole basis of the Christian life and offers life changing hope to subsequent disciples who may fail their Master."[65]

Discipleship is not really about us. Our understanding or obedience. It is about Jesus and His grace. His unfailing love. His promises and His faithfulness. When disciples fall, Jesus picks them up, brushes them off and sets them back on the path. Don't pretend you are not weak and do not fall. Without the ministry of the Holy Spirit, we would simply be as all unbelievers are. Hear John who later wrote,

"We proclaim to you what we have seen and heard, so that you also may have fellowship with us. And our fellowship is with the Father and with his Son , Jesus Christ.... This is the message we heard from him and declare to you: God is light; in him is no darkness at all. If we claim to have fellowship with him yet walk in darkness, we lie and do not live by the truth. But if we walk in the

light, as he is in the light, we have fellowship with one another, and the blood of Jesus, his Son, cleanses us from all sin.... If we confess our sins, he is faithful and justand will forgive us our sins and purify us from all unrighteousness" (1 John 1:3-9).

There is a walk with God and with one another. It is a life of discipleship. A step-by-step walking in the light. Jesus said, **"I am the light of the world. He that follows me will never walk in darkness, but will have the light of life."** (John 8:12). By faith, which the Holy Spirit alone can give, if you determine to never let anyone or anything between you and Jesus, then you will never walk in darkness. Start with a step right now. A command you have long laid aside. A neighbor you have avoided. A relative you have not reached out to. An offense you have not forgiven. You will never enjoy extensive deliverance from darkness until you enjoy the radiance of a single obedience. Take a trip with Jesus down the path you have refused to go. And you will discover that He is that real. He is that present. He delivers life to those disciples who submit to Him. Obey and live!

A 21ˢᵗ Century Disciple's Story

My name is Dan. I began following Jesus almost 5 years ago, after running from God while being an actor in New York City. In following Jesus, the hardest command for me to follow has been *a sacrifice of my free time*. I used to watch movies and sports all day long. This could easily take up 7-10 hours in a day between the two.

When I started to go down the road of becoming a disciple I quickly discovered that Jesus was asking me to spend my time in prayer and meeting people who were open to spiritual things. This was hard at first because it challenged my "relaxation time". Jesus was asking me to go out into the community. "Go and make disciples" he said. I took this to heart and started going.

And the results of obeying Jesus in love have been a straight up blessing in my life. I am meeting all kinds of people now in the community. I am discipling people! That's crazy! I still have free time and still watch some movies and sports. Just not 7-10 hours a day. It's all in balance AFTER making disciples. This is my life now.

My newly married wife has been a huge support for me and example, as she is "going" too! I am truly humbled that I get to "go" as a couple. We get to do this journey together. His favor and love is amazing! I can honestly say that the fruitfulness that we have seen is just the beginning of what God has in store for us.

The simplicity of "going" has changed my life. The result has been the emerging of disciples in my life. I am so thankful He told me to get up off the couch and go.

Quote from Andrew Murray

"Just as we have trusted Him as our Savior to atone for our disobedience, let us trust Him as our teacher to lead us out of it and into a life of practical obedience. It is the presence of Christ with us throughout each day that will keep us on the path of true commitment to our task.

"The path on which the Son himself learned obedience was long, and we must not wonder why it does not always come easily for us." (43)

Questions for Reflection

1. Why did the Bible's writers, when inspired by the Holy Spirit, give accounts of their own and other believers' worst sins?
2. What were some differences between how other rabbis called disciples and how Jesus did?
3. What were some of the sins and shortcomings of the apostles and why did Mark include them in his Gospel of Jesus?
4. Did this chapter encourage or discourage you to be a disciple of Jesus?

One-word Command to Obey

"Forgive"

If you **forgive** men when they sin against you, your heavenly Father will also **forgive** you. But if you do not **forgive** men their sins, your Father will not **forgive** your sins. (Matthew 6:14-15)

Lord, how many times shall I **forgive** my brother when he sins against me? Up to seven times? Jesus answered, I tell you, not seven times, but seventy-seven times… This is how my heavenly Father will treat each of you unless you **forgive** your brother from your heart. (Matthew 18:21,22,35)

And when you stand praying, if you hold anything against anyone, **forgive** him, so that your father in heaven may **forgive** you your sins. (Mark 11:25)

He said to them When you pray, say… **Forgive** us our sins, for we also **forgive** those who sin against us. (Luke 11:2,4)

If your brother sins, rebuke him, and if he repents **forgive** him. (Luke 17:3)

If you **forgive** anyone his sins, they are **forgiven**. (John 20:23)

Bear with each other and **forgive** whatever grievances you may have against one another. **Forgive** as the Lord forgave you. (Colossians 3:13)

"If they persecuted me, they will persecute you." (Jhn 15:20)

"Go! I am sending you out like lambs among wolves." (Luke 10:3)

"Do not suppose that I have come to bring peace to the earth. I did not come to bring peace, but a sword. For I have come to turn a man against his father, a daughter against her mother…a man's enemies will be the members of his own household. Anyone who loves father or mother more than me is not worthy of me; and anyone who does not take his cross and follow me is not worthy of me… Whoever loses his life for my sake will find it." (Matthew 10:34-39)

"I have…been in prison more frequently, been flogged more severely, and been exposed to death again and again. Five times I received from the Jews the forty lashes minus one. Three times I was beaten with rods, once I was pelted with stones, three times I was shipwrecked, I spent a night and a day in the open sea, I have been constantly on the move. I have been in danger from rivers, in danger from bandits, in danger from my fellow Jews, in danger from Gentiles; in danger in the city, in danger in the country, in danger at sea; and in danger from false believers. I have labored and toiled and have often gone without sleep; I have known hunger and thirst and have often gone without food; I have been cold and naked. Besides everything else, I face daily the pressure of my concern for all the churches." (2Corinthians 11:23-28)

"AD 31-33 – persecution begins. The apostles are flogged. That is, they are given the forty lashes minus one. The whip they are beaten with is called a scourge. It is made of 39 leather cords tied into 3 bands of 13 cords. The cords are weighted with pieces of bone and metal attached to a stout wooden handle. The apostles are whipped on the back and chest."

(Frank Viola, The Untold Story of the New Testament Church, p50)

Chapter Nine

The Apostles' Obedience – *Whatever the Cost*

This is the last chapter of a very focused book. My goal and prayer have been that you would become an obedient disciple of Jesus Christ who commits to making disciples. The type of follower Jesus described in His Great Commission: **"Teach them to obey everything I have commanded you."** You have, likely, NOT been discipled in this way by anyone. If you have, you are truly blessed![66] Please recognize that, even in the USA, many of you will represent a first generation of biblical discipleship when you start! So, you must begin on renewing the quality of your own walk with Jesus before you can help anyone else with theirs. Childlike obedience fired by love is a great way start.

Most of you have been taught, preached to, counseled and prayed for. You have attended Christian worship services, Sunday schools, prayer meetings, small groups, conferences, retreats and seminars. You have read books, listened to tapes, taken notes, watched Christian movies and tried to make sense of it all—applying some of them into your lives. Let me ask you—have you made ANY disciples as a result? Have you jumped off the log?

You see, obedience to Jesus, up to NOW, has probably remained an option for you. Plausible, but not necessary. What more possibly can I say to move you forward into obedience? I want to simply tell you the story of what happened to the bumbling, cowardly, run-for-the-hills apostles of Jesus when the Holy Spirit filled them. My prayer is that He will so fill you. My hope is that you will realize that He wants to fill you and flow through you. All of you, just as Paul commanded all of the Ephesians, **"Be filled with the Holy Spirit"** (Ephesians 5:18). The only way that you will be able to follow the apostles as they followed

Jesus is to be filled with the same Holy Spirit, who made their transformation and following possible.

In the last chapter, we left them re-gathering in Jerusalem to **"stay in the city until you have been clothed with power from on high"** (Luke 24:49). It took ten days. But when He came, **"all of them were filled with the Holy Spirit and began to speak in other tongues (languages) as the Spirit enabled them"** (Acts 2:4). The important point to remember was not that they spoke new languages, but that thousands of foreigners declared with amazement, **"they spoke the wonders of God in our own tongues!"** (Acts 2:11). Get this one simple truth. If you study the ten times in Acts that believers were "filled with the Holy Spirit,"[67] you will discover one and only one thing common to all. Whoever they were, wherever it might have happened, once they were filled with the Spirit, *they spoke about God*. They were filled and they spoke. A few times in unlearned languages. Normally, in their own mother-tongue. Acts 4:31 can be said to be representative of all instances of the Spirit's filling in Acts, **"And they were all filled with the Holy Spirit and spoke the**

word of God boldly." Boldly meant in a courageous way. The same way that they had seen and heard Jesus speak. By the prompting of the Spirit, who always filled Him.

It was in a very dangerous place and at a very dangerous time, after **"the Jews there (in Jerusalem) were waiting to take his life"** (John 7:1), and after **"the chief priests and the Pharisees sent temple guards to arrest him..."**(7:34), that the following occurred.

"On the last and greatest day of the Feast, Jesus stood up and said in a loud voice, 'If anyone is thirsty let him come to me and drink. Whoever believes in me, as the Scripture has said, 'Streams of living water will flow from within him.' By this he meant the Spirit, whom those who believed in him were later to receive. Up to this time the Spirit had not been given, since Jesus had not yet been glorified"(John 7:37-39).

No one is completely safe in this world when they let the Spirit flow through them. Those willing to be so used will be often misunderstood, misjudged, marginalized and opposed. Maybe even thrown out of the fellowship. Following Jesus and speaking as He did is risky business. A choice must be made. At the end of this chapter, you will have to make a choice. You cannot choose the way of Jesus for long unless you are filled with God. But, remember, that is not all!

"If I ... have not Love, I am Nothing" (1 Corinthians 13:2)

Please do not miss the cardinal truth that we have been reminding you of throughout this book: love matters most to God! So, whatever is not fueled by love is not fueled by the Holy Spirit. Consider the testimony of the New Testament. Love is the Spirit's first fruit (Galatians 5:22). It is that which He pours into the lives of all who are born again (Romans 5:5). Paul urged the Roman believers **"by our Lord Jesus Christ and by the love of the Spirit"** (Romans 15:30). Epaphras encouraged Paul by reporting that the Colossian believers were noted for their **"love in the Spirit"** (Colossians 1:8). As he concludes his short letter to all believers, Jude makes one command: "**Keep yourselves in God's love."**

And one of the three ways that he gave that would accomplish that goal is to **"pray in the Holy Spirit"** (Jude 20-21).

The apostles and their disciples were changed people because they were consumed with the love of Christ! The only way I will accomplish my goal of really helping you obey Jesus is by your being filled with the love of the Holy Spirit of God. Seek it and it will be yours. Let go of all other loves and make Him your "first love." **"If you, then, know how to give good gifts to your children, how much more will your Father give the Holy Spirit to those who ask him!"** (Luke 11:13). I want you to be something great for Jesus and His Kingdom. Without love, no matter how strenuously you work at it, you will **"gain nothing"** (1 Corinthians 13:3b).[68]

Apostolic "first love"

So, read carefully now the story of how deeply the apostles loved Jesus after He ascended. When, as we have seen, they lived by faith in His presence. For it is only as you are filled with the same Spirit as they were filled with that you can have the same love for Jesus that they had. And then follow the same Jesus whom they followed. For **"Jesus Christ is the same yesterday, today and forever"** (Hebrews 13:8). What you will notice now is that the law of self-preservation, which is one of the strongest instincts within us all—must be conquered by love. And **"love never seeks its own"** (1 Corinthians. 13:5-NKJV). In following Jesus, we must have His love in us. The love that jumps on the grenade for the battalion around you. Of which Jesus said, **"Greater love has no one than this, that he lay down his life for his friends"** (John 13:13).

You will quickly see three things. First, true love is a beautiful thing. No cost is considered when love is brought into the equation. All that matters is that the beloved knows that he or she is loved. But, secondly, true love is a costly thing, too. For it demands not only your wealth, but your very self. And so, as Jesus said, **"If anyone would come after me, he must deny himself and take up his cross daily and follow me"** (Luke 9:23). You must say, "NO!" to yourself and take up your cross daily. It is in the embracing of suffering, for Jesus and the gospel, that your love, like the apostles, will be proven to be true. And that suffering may take very different shapes. It will be your "cup to drink," and no one else's. That was the lesson Peter learned when Jesus told him Peter would die an awful death. And Peter, looking at John, said, **"what about him?"** To which Jesus replied, **"If I want him to remain alive until I return, what is that to you? You must follow me"** (John 21:21-22). John had his cross to bear, too. But it was different from Peter's. You prove your love for Jesus when your cross does not mean more to you than He means to you. When your love for Him conquers your fears of the cost of following Him. Or as Spurgeon once said, "It is a blessed mark of growth out of spiritual infancy when we can forego the joys which once appeared to be essential, and can find our solace in Him who denies them to us."[69]

When all the Apostles Proved their Love

We focus a lot on the first few chapters of Acts where we see the ascension of Jesus, the waiting in "the upper room," Pentecost and the Church's first great ingathering of 3,000 men (not yet counting women and children— that would come!), the healing of the lame man and the additional mass conversion of 2,000 more men. This crescendos into Peter and John's showdown with the Sanhedrin. It is recorded in Acts 4. They were now at the mercy of those who had arrested, abused and crucified Jesus. How did the apostles feel? What were they thinking about as their wives and children flashed through their minds? Not to mention the 20,000 disciples who, by this time, constituted the young Jerusalem church? We cannot know what they felt. We can only know what they did, for often obedience comes at the expense of feelings!

"Then Peter, filled with the Holy Spirit, said to them...." (4:8). The Sanhedrin did not like what he said. After they had told them to leave the room, the discussion went like this,

"What are we going to do with these men? Everybody living in Jerusalemknows they have done an outstanding miracle, and we cannot deny it. But to stop this thing from spreading any further among the people, we must warn these men to speak no longer in this name." (Acts 4:16-17).

So they **"commanded them not to speak or teach at all in the name of Jesus. But "Peter and John replied, 'Judge for yourselves whether it is right in God's sight to obey you rather than God. For we cannot help speaking about what we have seen and heard"** (4:18-20).

The Sanhedrin, taken aback by such a response, **"could not decide how to punish them,"** and so released them. The love of God cannot be silenced by threats. Even by those who have proven that they will go to any extreme to violently silence their opponents.

Hurray, we shout! Like keeping the score, we think, Church 1- Sanhedrin 0. We get so caught up with the miracles and the boldness that we forget the price all the apostles were called on to pay. This is found in a single verse that we often overlook. In fact, I did not even remember this ever taking place! I was so caught up in the various stories Luke mentions that this one sentence did not register.

Did you know that there was a time when all the apostles were imprisoned at the same time? Luke wrote, **"They arrested the**

apostles and put them in the public jail." (Acts 5:18). Not just Peter and John—all of the apostles. There they are. In jail, with their haters plotting their demise in a nearby room. But, all power has been given to Jesus in heaven and in earth! And to those who go and make disciples, He promised **"I, myself am with you to the end of the age."** As we read the story in Acts 5:17-42, we see it reveals:

-That very night an angel of the Lord opened the doors of the jail

-The angel brought them out and said, **"Go and stand in the temple courts and tell thepeople the full message of this new life"** (v. 20).

-So, at daybreak, they did! Returning to where they had been told not to go and saying what they had been told not to say.

-The high priest and Sanhedrin, after comfortably sleeping in their own beds, regathered in full assembly at the Temple to try the apostles. They sent for them and found no one inside the locked jail doors even though the guards were at the entrance!

-While in confusion, someone breaks into the room and proclaims, "**Look! The men you put in jail are standing in the temple courts teaching the people!**"

-The apostles are re-arrested and brought before the gathered leaders, who did not ask them how they escaped, but only, "**We gave you strict orders not to teach in this name, yet you have filled Jerusalem with your teaching and are determined to make us guilty of this man's blood**" (v. 28).

-Peter and the other apostles boldly reply, "**We must obey God rather than men! The God of our fathers raised Jesus from the dead—whom you killed by hanging him on a tree... We are witnesses of these things, and so is the Holy Spirit, whom God has given to those who obey him.**" (5:29-32)

Did you get that? WE MUST OBEY GOD! To whom is the Holy Spirit given? **"To those who obey him."** You quickly reveal how many MUSTS are in your life when you face such men. People will want to silence you. When they get you to deny Jesus, they think they have won. That you are just like them. That you can be bought or persuaded to forsake all this Christian foolishness.

-On hearing this, **"they were furious and wanted to put them to death"** (v. 33).

-Gamaliel, the most renowned rabbi of his day, barely restrained them from executing the whole band of apostles. But these men must be shown who is in charge. They must be punished.

-So, **"they called the apostles in and had them flogged. Then they ordered them not to speak in the name of Jesus, and let them go"** (v. 40).

-**"The apostles left the Sanhedrin, rejoicing because they had been**

counted worthy of suffering disgrace for the Name" (5:42).

These apostles had been discipled by Jesus. They were His followers. He said they would suffer. They would daily bear a cross. And, as they had been formed, so they were to make other disciples. Followers of Jesus who could suffer for Him. And then rejoice. How do you do when you suffer for Jesus? How strongly do you rejoice? Have you ever really suffered for Jesus?

I need to explain to you what these words meant for the apostles, **"they...had them flogged."** While this is graphically depicted, please remember, only the filling of the Spirit can make men endure this willingly, obediently and joyfully. This entire episode is impossible to fathom apart from one truth—they were all filled with the love of Jesus, who had taught them, **"whoever has my commands and obeys them, he is the one who loves me."** (John 14:21). Love obeys Jesus.

Suffering Disgrace for the Name

No one can look at Paul's list of sufferings, with which I introduced this chapter, and think that he was anything other than an idiot or a saint. That he was either deceived or enlightened. Though many of us are protected by laws ensuring freedom of religion, they were not. Why were the apostles flogged? Why didn't they cut a deal with the Sanhedrin? Why didn't they just devote themselves to a benign, lifestyle evangelism that offended no one? Because Jesus had commanded them to go, to preach, to make disciples. He promised them, **"You will receive power when the Holy Spirit comes on you; and you will be my witnesses in Jerusalem…."** (Acts 1:8). Even when Jerusalem's leaders did not want to hear His name, they must speak. Even if it meant…**flogging.**

I now turn to an expert researcher on New Testament times. I hope that such graphic accounting will increase your understanding and admiration of the apostles and all those who TODAY suffer as disciples of Jesus.

"What were the "thirty-nine lashes?" In fact, 'forty stripes less one' were sometimes fatal. It was a type of beating employed only among the Jewish religious community. Its purpose was to bring an erring Hebrew back to the orthodox views of Judaism, that is, back to the teaching of Moses and, the traditions of the elders. It was a severe punishment administered to bring the accused to repentance. It had probably been invented as a last ditch show of mercy to be used on a man in place of stoning him to death.

"To be sentenced to this lashing was the most shameful thing that could happen to a Jew. It brought shame not only upon him but also upon his entire family. In that day a man apparently would have done anything to escape the physical agony and the social humiliation of these stripes. That was about to change...and suddenly! The followers of Jesus Christ showed no sign of shame. Instead, they stood there rejoicing! It was very unnerving...and probably unprecedented in all human history.

"The disciple listens to the sentence…. He is led to stand between two marble columns. His hands are spread apart and tied to the pillars. Then his back is stripped bare. A few feet behind him someone places a stand. Another man… the 'hazzan' steps uponto the stand, he unrolls a heavy whip. The whip has four strips of leather on it, each about three or four feet long. Two of these leather strips are of calf's hide, the other two are from the hide of a donkey.

"The hazzan, standing on the small raised platform, turns slowly around toward the barred back of the disciple. The disciple cannot seethe proceedings, but knows what is about to happen. The hazzan raises the whip high into the air, straightens and then brings it down with all his might.

"The whip does not land on the disciple's back, but rather, on the top of his shoulders. The leather strips reach out beyond his shoulders, falling hard upon his chest and stomach. The blow instantly causes welts and bruises all over his chest and stomach. The hazzan quickly pulls the whip back with a jerk and the leather rakes back over the bruised skin.

"There is a pause. Again the whip goes high into the air, and again it comes straight down upon the disciple's shoulders. This time the leather lands upon tender, swollen skin. With each blow the disciple's skin becomes more bruised. The welts begin opening and finally turn into open gashes. After even more blows, the leather starts finding its way into the bone of the rib cage. Each blow is like coals of burning fire upon the chest.

"The disciple receives thirteen such lashes across his front. At this point he is probably already in shock, dehydrated and nearly delirious with pain. The inquisitor now begins the second thirteen lashes, aiming them at the back. Thirteen slashes of leather find their way across the right side of the disciple's back, each furrowing deeper into the flesh than the one before.

"By now the disciple is probably semi-conscious and on the verge of fainting. His muscle coordination is lost. No longer able to stand, he now swings from the cords binding him to the marble pillars. And there are still thirteen more lashes to come. These make their permanent mark on his left side.

"At last it is over. This brave believer, probably unconscious and close to death, is cut down and dragged out. ... The disciple has made it through the ordeal. He did not deny his Lord, and he had the glorious privilege of fellowship in the sufferings of his Lord. ... When he awakened, his body would be on fire and he would have an unquenchable thirst. Moving would be agony. Ahead of him would be weeks of slow healing and intense pain. Across his chest, across his stomach and across his back he would carry deep furrowed scars as trophies of his love for his Lord."[70]

Open the door

All the Christians around me say that they want to be "biblical." The church planters want to plant "New Testament churches." Churches that are "Pauline" in their likeness. Seminarians want to pick and choose where they will "serve the Lord." What they will be paid. The benefit package they will enjoy. Those who are "called to the mission field" spend two years raising funds. Once they get there, if their funding drops below 80% they are "called back" until they "raise what they need." The apostles and the Early Church would hardly recognize what today is being done in the name of Christianity. Jesus told the Laodicean church,

"You say, I am rich; I have acquired wealth and do not need a thing.' But you do not realize that you are wretched, pitiful, poor, blind and naked. I counsel you to buy from me gold refined in the fire... Those whom I love I rebuke and discipline.

So be earnest, and repent. Here I am! I stand at the door and knock, if anyone hears my voice and opens the door, I will come in and eat with him, and he with me" (Revelation 3:17-20).

Could Jesus be calling YOU through this chapter? Is He knocking at YOUR door? Remember, it was to the CHURCH in Laodicea that these words were written. To a first century church! A church of Christ! YOU, likely, belong to a 21st century church of Christ. Is it time for you to open the door again? This time all the way! In true repentance. In true self denial. He that has ears to hear, let him hear.

"Follow me as I follow Christ"

Paul was an apostle of Jesus. He described himself as **"the least of the apostles and do not even deserve to be called an apostle, because I persecuted the church of God"** (1 Corinthians 15:9). As an apostle, he went to Corinth and **"laid a foundation as an expert builder"** (3:10). He warned them that **"each one should be careful how he builds. For no one can lay any foundation other than the one already laid, which is**

Jesus Christ" (3:10-11). Then he told them, **"follow my example as I follow the example of Christ"** (11:1).

Whom are you following? And who is following you? Are you following Jesus? And can others know that they will be following Jesus as they follow you? THAT, simply put, was **"the apostles' teaching"** (Acts 2:42). The pattern and chief example is always Jesus. The suffering-to-glory Jesus. The cross-to-crown Jesus. The dying-that-others-might-live Jesus. Can't you see that dying to yourself is not the crowning achievement of a long-lived Christian life? It is the first step. We die that we might live. **"For whoever wants to save his life will lose it, but whoever loses his life for me will save it"** (Luke 9:24). **"Whoever"** is you and me. **"Saving our lives"** is grasping on to them and not letting go. **"Losing our lives"** is letting go of ourselves, dying to ourselves, denying ourselves.

Hear again, but maybe as if it were the first time, the famous and often-quoted words of the martyr Dietrich Bonhoeffer, "… the cross is not the terrible end to an otherwise God-fearing and happy life, but it meets us at the beginning of our communion with Christ. When Christ calls a man, he bids him come and die."[71] Was Bonhoeffer telling the truth or a lie? Is there another way? Can you build your life on **"the foundation of the apostles and prophets"** and produce a totally different looking building? A comfortable, lavish living and sparsely giving, American-dream-or-bust, Christian life? Is there really ANY place for a constantly disobedient Christian? A Christian who refuses to submit and obey Jesus Christ? There may be room TODAY in the churches, but the time is coming when such delusion will be totally destroyed.

> **"God is just… This will happen when the Lord Jesus is revealed from heaven in blazing fire with his powerful angels. He will punish those who … do not obey the gospel of our Lord Jesus"** (2 Thessalonians 1:6-8).

Obedience to Jesus is not optional. There is no true Christianity except that which is based on the foundation of New Testament discipleship. Remember, **"the disciples were called Christians first at Antioch"** (Acts 11:26). They were first disciples and then they were called Christians! You might call yourself a Christian today, but that does not make you one. Whose disciple are you? Who has control over your life? To whom do you belong? Do these quotes from Bonhoeffer echo the teaching, preaching, reading and reflecting that your life has been built upon? If not, then, please question the foundation!

> -Cheap grace is the deadly enemy of our Church. We are fighting today for costly grace.[72]

> -Cheap grace is grace without discipleship, grace without the cross, without Jesus Christ, living and incarnate.[73]

> -Costly grace is the treasure hidden in the field; for the sake of it a man will gladly go and sell all that he has. It is the pearl of great price....It is the kingly rule of Christ, for whose sake a man will pluck out the eye which causes him to stumble; it is the call of Jesus Christ at which the disciple leaves his nets and follows him...Such grace is costly because it calls us to follow, and it is grace because it calls us to follow

Jesus Christ. It is costly because it costs a man his life, and it is grace because it gives a man the only true life.[74]

-As Christianity spread, and the Church became more secularized, this realization of the costliness of grace gradually faded. The world was Christianized, and grace became its common property. It was to be had at low cost.[75]

-The word of cheap grace has been the ruin of more Christians than any commandment ofworks.[76]

-Discipleship means adherence to Christ, and, because Christ is the object of that adherence, it must take the form of discipleship. An abstract Christology... renders discipleship superfluous... Christianity without the living Christ, is inevitably Christianity without discipleship, and Christianity without discipleship is always Christianity withoutChrist.[77]

-Only he who believes is obedient, and only he who is obedient believes.[78]

-Unbelief thrives on cheap grace, for it is determined to persist in disobedience.[79]

-To deny oneself is to be aware only of Christ and no more of self, to see only him who goes before and no more the road which is too hard forus. Once more, all that self-denial can say is: "He leads the way, keep close to him."[80]

Why did Paul Return?

As we move on from the apostles to the churches they established, we see that they demanded of their new disciples the same level of obedience to Jesus and willingness to suffer for Him that they, themselves, were committed to. That is what being built on their foundation looked like. The belief and behavior of the third-generation disciples mirrored that of the apostles.[81] Willingness to suffer for God was the in-born DNA of those disciples. We see this so clearly when Paul returned to the churches he had planted under severe persecution on his first missionary journey.

"Then some Jews came from Antioch and Iconium, and won the crowd over. They stoned Paul and dragged him outside the city, thinking he was dead. But after thedisciples had gathered around him, he got up and went back into the city. The next day he and Barnabas left for Derbe. They preached the good news in that city and won a large number of disciples. Then they returned to Lystra, Iconium and Antioch strengthening the disciples and encouraging them to remain true to the faith(saying), 'We must go through many hardships to enter the kingdom of God.'"
(Acts 14:19-22).

Marvel at the beauty and truth of this narrative!

-Paul was stoned (and you thought **flogging** was bad!), yet he returned into the city and spent the night rather than running for his life

-In Derbe, Paul preached the gospel and made disciples! He did not make believers who prayed with every head bowed and every eye closed. Secret believers. No. The result of his gospel-preaching was open, fully committed discipleship. Those disciples would have heard the call of Jesus to come, deny themselves, take up their crosses and follow Him. Because that is how LUKE always used the word "disciple" in both Luke and Acts. Disciples were made at the moment of baptism. By faith, they embraced the death of Jesus (and their own death to sin) that they might live.

-Paul and Barnabas then returned to the cities where they had been horrendously persecuted. Were they nuts? Why go back and risk the same again? They were already dead men who lived in and for Christ and His Church!

-The message that they gave to the disciples, which so encouraged them, was that they must ready themselves for much tribulation. They must bear their own crosses! And Luke said this "**encouraged**" them! How encouraged would USA Christians be to THAT message? If a pastor dared to live and preach it in many of the churches I know—he better have his bags packed.

So, let us answer the question, "Why did Paul return?" Because he was a disciple maker who modeled for his disciples how to follow Jesus in times of acceptance and suffering. He proved to them that **"all things** (even beatings and stonings) **work together for good to those who love God"** (Romans 8:28 – NKJV).

Why did Paul Wait?

Many of you may know the story of Paul and Silas at Philippi. It is during his second missionary journey and just followed his "Macedonian Vision" that led him and his mission team into Europe for the first time (Acts 16:6-10). When arriving at Philippi, he finds a very small Jewish population. There were not even enough Jewish males to start a synagogue, so they met at **"a place of prayer"** by the riverside. A woman named Lydia believed and became a disciple, inviting Paul and the team to stay with her.[82]

On one of the trips to the place of prayer, Paul was met by a demonized girl, whom he delivered from the demon. Pick up this important event with me,

"When the owners of the slave girl realized that their hope of making money was gone, they seized Paul and Silas and dragged them into the marketplace to face the authorities.... The crowd joined in the attack against Paul and Silas, and the magistrates ordered them to be stripped and beaten. After they had been severely flogged[83], they were thrown into prison, and the jailer was commanded to guard them carefully. Upon receiving such orders, he put them in the inner cell and fastened their feet with stocks. "About midnight Paul and Silas were praying and singing hymns to God, and the other prisoners were listening to them. Suddenly there was such a violent earthquake that the foundations of the prison were shaken. At once all the prison doors flew open

and everyone's chains came loose." (Acts 16:19-26).

The jailer immediately draws a sword **"to kill himself because he thought that the prisoners had escaped"** (v. 27). At which time Paul shouts out for him not to harm himself as they are all still in the prison. The jailer gets a torch, and **"trembling before Paul and Silas ... asked, 'What must I do to be saved?'"** (v. 30). He and his household believe, the jailer washes their wounds and they are immediately baptized.

"When it was daylight, the magistrates sent their officers to the jailer with the order, 'Release those men.'" Then they got the surprise and fright of their lives. Paul told the magistrates that they "**beat us publicly without a trial, even though we were Roman citizens**" (v. 37). So, Paul was not going to go away quietly. He wanted to make a point and secure the safety of the fledgling Philippian church plant. Paul had them in a tight spot because the magistrates could have been severely punished for their mistreatment of Roman citizens.

One obvious question is begging to be asked, "Paul, why did you wait until after your beating to let the magistrates know you are a Roman citizen?" Human instinct would cry out, "Civis Romanus sum" (I am a Roman citizen). Instead they are severely beaten with birch rods, thrown into jail and had their ankles secured in iron shackles. And how do they respond? They are singing songs of praise to God! And what happens? An earthquake, a converted jailer and his family (not to mention how the prisoners had been impressed), the growth and securing of safety for the church!

Somehow Paul and Silas knew that the door of suffering would better establish the church in Philippi than crying out for their own release. What madness! Yes, thinking logically and bearing in mind the instinct of self-preservation, it is insane. But these men were disciples of Jesus. And Jesus had taught, **"I tell you the truth, unless a kernel of wheat falls to the ground and dies, it remains only a single seed. But if it dies, it produces many seeds. The man who loves his life will lose it, while the man who hates his life will keep it for eternal life."** (John 12:24-25). Somehow the Holy Spirit had convinced Paul and Silas to ride it out by faith and see His mighty, saving work! Is that the foundation upon which our belief and behavior are based?

Can You Sing this Hymn?

Paul belonged to Jesus. And he always urged his disciples to live similarly. When Timothy was wavering, in Paul's last biblical letter, he wrote to his beloved son in the faith,

"You then my son, be strong in the grace that is in Christ Jesus.... Endure hardship with us like a good soldier of Christ Jesus.... Remember Jesus Christ, raised from the dead, descended from David. This is my gospel, for which I am suffering even to the point of being chained like a criminal. But God's word is not chained. Therefore I endure everything for the sake of God's elect, that they too may obtain the salvation that is in Christ Jesus, with eternal glory. Here is a trustworthy saying:

**If we died with him, we will also live with him.
If we endure, we will also reign with him.
If we disown him, he also will disown us;
If we are faithless, he will remain faithful, he cannot disownhimself."
(2 Timothy 2:1-13)**

Many scholars have concluded that Paul's "saying" was probably an early church hymn. Sung by faithful disciples as they gathered for worship and as they lived day by day. You will end reading this book well if you will believe, memorize and sing that discipleship hymn throughout life.

Filling and Obedience

As we conclude this book and our focus on following Christ as the apostles did, there is an important exclamation mark we must leave. We have noted our absolute need to be constantly filled with the Holy Spirit. But, you must understand that they would NOT have been filled with the Spirit if they had not obeyed Jesus! Or put positively, they were filled with the Spirit because they followed Jesus! Not perfectly in every step they took — but sufficiently, by a living faith. And their faith did not look to Jesus merely to give them knowledge of the way to walk, or **what to do.** Their faith fastened on Jesus to empower them, or help them with **how to do.** Paul understood this when he concluded, **"I can do all things through Christ who strengthens me"** (Philippians 4:13 – NKJV).

One of my accountability partners, Gene, shared a verse with me TODAY, that helped open this truth to me. We know that the apostles boldly confessed to the Sanhedrin, **"We must obey God rather than men!"** (Acts 5:29). But I had forgotten how they closed that brave witness before Christ's enemies. Read this carefully: **"We are witnesses of these things, and so is the Holy Spirit, whom God has given to those who obey him"** (Acts 5:32). That might be new truth to you. The Spirit is specially given to those who obey Jesus. Here is the biblical chronology:

1. The resurrected Jesus said, " **'Peace be with you! As the Father has sent me, I am sending you.' And with that he breathed on them and said, 'Receive the Holy Spirit.' "** (John 20:21). So, the apostles had the Spirit, but NOT His later, special filling.

2. Jesus told them after this and just before He ascended, **"Stay in the city until you have been clothed with power from on high"** (Luke 24:49). He had been with them, after His resurrection "forty days" (Acts 1:3).

3. When Jesus was ascending into heaven and blessing them, the apostles **worshiped him and returned to Jerusalem with great joy. And they stayed continually at the temple praising God" (Luke 24:52-53).**

4. The Spirit gave them faith and grace to OBEY Jesus and return to Jerusalem. To go back to the most dangerous city on earth to them. And they went to the temple, the center of their deadliest opponents' ministries.

5. They were staying in an upper room where **"they all joined constantly in prayer, along with the women and Mary the mother of Jesus, and with his brothers"** (Acts 2:14). How can you be in constant prayer, true prayer, without the help of the Spirit?

6. Peter was led to stand and teach from the Word about Judas' betrayal and concluded **"it is necessary to choose one of the men who have been with us the whole time the Lord Jesus went in and out among us, beginning from John's baptism to the time when Jesus was taken from us"** (Acts 1:15-22).

They prayed to Jesus (v 24) and asked Him to choose the successor of Judas Iscariot. **"And the lot fell to Matthias, so he was added to the eleven apostles."** (Acts 1:26). This whole prayerful choosing of Judas' replacement, restoring the number to twelve and assuring that every apostle had a partner, was obviously empowered by the Spirit.

7. Then, after ten days of waiting, on the day of Pentecost, **"they were all together inone place. Suddenly a sound like the blowing of a violent wind came from heaven and filled the whole house where they were staying... All of them were filled with the Holy Spirit and began to speak in other languages as the Spirit enabled them"** (Acts 2:1-4). The Spirit filled them as they had **obediently** gone to Jerusalem and waited for the filling, which was a new level of empowerment. They had the wonderful influence of the Spirit prior to Pentecost, or they could not have done what they did. But they were not filled or empowered to the same degree which they experienced at Pentecost and daily thereafter.

So, we must understand that simple obedience to Jesus, to following Him and living as He has directed us in His Word, is a necessary pre-requisite to be filled with the Spirit. The Spirit will not fill a disobedient vessel. He may indwell one. But He will not fill one. When we are filled, He flows from us with great power and love.

It makes great sense, then, why Paul warned the Ephesians, **"do not grieve the Holy Spirit of God"** (4:30), and shortly after commanded them to "**be filled with the Spirit."** The Spirit will not fill us when He is grieved by us. Sins, as those listed in chapter 4, grieve the Spirit and keep us from being filled. It does not surprise any of us that **unholiness** grieves the **Holy** Spirit. Disobedience is one type of unholiness. Obedience, from the heart of faith and love, is a sure mark of holiness.

But the filling must be sought. We must actively pray for His filling, repenting of any and every sin that might be hindering our filling. We must not be satisfied with the forms of morality or spirituality that most Christians are satisfied with. No! Disciples want to follow Jesus and, as we are going, to make other disciples in His name!

Spirit, help us to obey what we know, what we have refused to obey, so that we might be truly **a vessel for honor, sanctified and useful for the Master, prepared for every good work"** (2 Timothy 2:21-NKJV). You are the source of our every obedience, dear

Spirit of God. Without You, the Spirit of Jesus, we cannot take a single step. But we want to do more than take one step. We want to perpetually follow. Fill us so that we might truly be **"living sacrifices, holy and pleasing to God"** (Romans 12:1). Fill us and flow through us for the glory of Jesus and the advancement of His Kingdom!

Will YOU Follow Jesus?

I hope that I have made the case that every Christian needs to be a disciple.[84] And that every disciple needs to prove the authenticity of his or her relationship with Jesus by a life of loving obedience. So the question, "Will you follow?" really asks, *"Will you obey Jesus?"* I pray so with Paul's own words, **"May the God who gives endurance and encouragement give you a spirit of unity among yourselves as you follow Christ Jesus, so that with one heart and mouth you may glorify the God and Father of our Lord Jesus Christ"** (Romans 15:5).

Make sure you read the appendices in which you will find help in identifying those commands of Jesus that have direct reference to all His disciples throughout all ages and cultures—until He comes. Come, Lord Jesus![85]

A 21st Century Disciple's Story

My name is Sue. When Jesus renewed my call to follow Him, the hardest obedience He demanded of me was *to give up financial stability*. Earlier in our lives, we could pay our bills on time and have money left over. My husband had a thriving IT business. I was (and am) a preschool teacher. We had challenges, but life felt pretty good.

Then the economy changed. We learned we owed more on the mortgage than our home was worth. We also learned first-hand the truth of Jesus' words in Matthew 7:24. Part of our house had been built on sand. The back began to pull away from the rest of the house. We were facing a very stressful economic and domestic situation.

Another effect of the economic downturn was that my husband lost most of his clients as small business owners had to cut back on computer support. Neither finding new clients nor looking for another job worked. The stress of our financial situation was heightening.

During that time Fred attended what Ed Gross now calls a "Renewal of Biblical Discipleship." He also attended a three-day discipleship training that CityTeam International offered. He was fired up, eager to make disciples. He got started right away, pouring himself into this new calling from God. He quickly became a leader in our area. After I attended the same trainings, I was ready to join him. God brought many people to us. They wanted to make disciples but had no idea how to get started. So we began to train them. It became evident that Fred had neither the time nor the opportunity to earn a living in IT. So what were we going to do?

Jesus was asking us to follow, to trust Him. Financial support began to trickle in, but it wasn't anywhere near the amount we needed. Unpaid bills caused great anxiety for me. However, God was at work in my heart. Daily I said, "Today I have a house that stands, all the utilities still on, food, clothes, medical coverage, and a car with gas in it." Our needs were being met. In situation after situation God proved His faithfulness by providing what we needed.

We needed to move out of the house while we figured out what to do with it. Where would we go? Not one, but three generous couples offered us a home with them. We moved into a positive situation. We are continuing to serve our awesome God. Come and follow Jesus with us.

Quotes from Andrew Murray

"Adam is the type of Him who was to come—the Second Adam, the Second Father of the race. Adam's disobedience in its effect is the exact similitude of what the obedience of Christ becomes to us. When a sinner believes in Christ, he is united to Him and by a judicial sentence is at once pronounced and accepted as righteous in God's sight. ...He has Christ's righteousness only by having Christ himself and being in Him....

"The one thing God asked of Adam in the Garden was obedience. The one thing by which a creature can glorify God or enjoy His favor and blessing is obedience. The single cause of the power of sin in the world and the ruin it has caused is disobedience. From Adam we have inherited a tendency to willfulness, to selfishness, to disobedience....

"...Christ overcame disobedience and gives us the power to replace ours with His obedience" (23-25)

Questions for Reflection

1. Discuss the importance of love's connection with our obedience. What happens when love is absent?
2. Discuss what you think would likely happen if most Christians you know were given the ultimatum and the threat of flogging that the apostles faced. WHY do you think this?
3. Which of the Bonhoeffer quotes surprised or touched you most?
4. Discuss what would likely occur if Paul's "encouraging" message given to the churches in Acts 14 was delivered to your church and the churches you know.
5. Why did Paul wait to tell the magistrates that he and Silas were Roman citizens?
6. Will you memorize the early hymn and follow Jesus?
7. Discuss how Acts 5:32 impacted you.

One-word Command to Obey

"Be strong" or "Strengthen"

When you have turned back, **strengthen** your brothers. (Luke 22:32)

Then the church…was **strengthened** and encouraged by the Holy Spirit, it grew in numbers, living in the fear of the Lord. (Acts 9:31)

Strengthening the disciples and encouraging them to remain true to the faith. (Acts 14:22)

Paul… traveled from place to place **strengthening** all the disciples. (Acts 18: 23)

Be on your guard. Stand firm in the faith. Be men of courage; **be strong**. (1 Corinthians 16:13)

Be strong in the Lord and in his mighty power. (Ephesians 6:10)

Be strong in the grace that is in Christ Jesus. (2 Timothy 2:1)

Therefore **strengthen** your feeble arms and weak knees. (Hebrews 12:12)

It is good for our hearts to be **strengthened** by grace. (Hebrews 13:9)

Strengthen what remains and is about to die. (Revelation 3:2)

Appendices

Appendix One – The Commands of Jesus in Mark's Gospel

The Scriptures must be interpreted, as much as possible, within their own original settings. Commands should not be snatched out of context and demanded of us or others for whom the Lord never intended them. The Spirit is our best Teacher[86] and will **"guide us into all truth."** He **"convicts of sin"** and strengthens us to repent and turn to Jesus in obedience. And He does that in His own inimitable way through the Word, our consciences and others' words.

Although the Spirit works as He will, it is good to have some guidelines about interpreting the commands of Jesus and the apostles. In the Introduction to his very helpful and readable book, *The Commands of Christ*, Tom Blackaby gives the following advice:

"Not all of Christ's teachings are what we might technically consider to be *command*s. Here are some general categories into which His teachings can be divided. (Examples are provided.)

1. General Observations (Luke 12:34; 16:13)
2. Warnings (Luke 12:10)
3. Commands (Matt. 5:16; 6:33 Luke 6:30)
4. Conversations (the woman at the well - John 4)
5. Teachings/Lessons (Parables like the sower and the seed Luke 8 and John 14:6).

"Whether we would actually consider Christ's teachings or conversations or observations (to be) 'commands,' we should keep in mind that God does not give His people suggestions. Whatever proceeds out of the mouth of the Father, the Son, or the Spirit is ... important and authoritative to the Christian life regardless of how we might want to classify it....

"Not all of the commands of Christ are necessarily intended for every believer forall time. Some were given for specific people in a particular situation."[87]

Blackaby broadly classifies Jesus' commands into six general areas (Coming to God, Christ as Lord, Character, Concerning Others, Calling and Cautions). He then lists and comments on 50 specific commands in these six general areas. He concludes with an epilogue on "Following Christ's Commands is an Act of Love." Blackaby's and other such books are a good resource for disciples who really want to obey everything Jesus has commanded.

Recently I read through Mark's Gospel, looking only for the commands of Jesus. I did this during my morning Bible readings with reflection and prayer. It was a very valuable spiritual exercise during which the Holy Spirit greatly instructed, convicted and helped me. I would recommend every disciple going through the Word in such a way.

In my prayerful study, this is what I found. There are 130 commands of Jesus recorded in Mark. The commands were given to 33 different individuals, groups of individuals, demons and even objects in the natural world. So, it is obvious, that not all of these commands are intended for us as individuals or groups today. But there are many of them that are timeless and cross-culturally valid. As New Testament scholar, Prof. Larry Hurtado, when considering Mark's Gospel, wrote,

> "Within the story of Jesus, the disciples function primarily as a model of what is involved in being a member of Jesus' people....They serve the important function, both positively and negatively, of showing the readers of the Gospel just what is involved in being a follower of Jesus and a beneficiary of his saving activity. Encouraging readers tobecome disciples in this sense is one of the major goals of the author as he goes about telling the story."[88]

So, the commands of Jesus, though largely issued to individuals and groups in the first century, were designed by Mark to help us all understand and navigate our own road of discipleship as we follow Jesus in subsequent generations and centuries. It does not take a great deal of wisdom to discern which commands are time-bound and limited and which are timeless and unlimited in their scope. In Mark's Gospel, 25 of the latter, always relating to us, are:

"Repent and believe the good news!" (1:15)

"Come, follow me and I will make you fishers of men." (1:17)

"He who has ears to hear, let him hear." (4:18)

"Consider carefully what you hear." (concerning Christ's teaching – 4:24)

"Go in peace" (5:34)

"Don't be afraid. Just believe." (5:36)

"Take courage. Don't be afraid." (6:48)

"If anyone would come after me, he MUST deny himself and take up his cross and follow me." (8:34)

"Do not stop him...for whoever is not against us is for us." (9:39)

"Have salt among yourselves and be at peace with each other." (9:50)

"What God has joined together, let man not separate." (10:6)

"Let the little children come to me, and do not hinder them." (10:14)

"Not so with you. Instead, whoever wants to be great among you must be your servant, and whoever wants to be first must be slave to all." (10:43-44)

"Have faith in God." (11:22)

"Therefore I tell you, whatever you ask for in prayer, believe that you have received it, and it will be yours." (11:24)

"And when you stand praying, if you hold anything against anyone, forgive him, so that your Father in heaven may forgive your sins." (11:25)

"Love the Lord your God with all your heart and with all your soul and with all your mind and with all your strength. The second is this: Love your neighbor as yourself." (12:30-31)

"And the gospel must be preached to all nations." (Mark 13:10)

"Be on guard! Be alert!" (13:33)

"Therefore keep watch because you do not know when the owner of the house will come back.... If he comes suddenly do not let him find you sleeping. What I say to you, I say to everyone, Watch!" (13:35-37)

"Take it, this is my body. Then he took the cup, gave thanks and offered it to them, and they all drank from it." (14:22-23)

"Watch and pray so that you will not fall into temptation. The spirit is willing, butthe body is weak." (14:38)

"Go into all the world and preach the gospel to all creation." (16:15)

Disciples filled with the Holy Spirit will relish discovering for themselves such simple commands throughout the Word of God. In the other Gospel accounts there are more speeches of Jesus recorded in which there are many more commands that He gave to His disciples.

Appendix Two

35 Commands of Jesus in "The Sermon on the Mount"

Many scholars have seen Jesus' "Sermon on the Mount" as an excellent introduction to His school of discipleship. The great Bible teacher, G. Campbell Morgan (1863-1945), wrote,

> "The Sermon on the Mount…was delivered specially to the disciples….Men have hardly begun to guess at the glory and beauty of this wonderful ideal, but in relation to the Teacher it is elementary and initial…. Here He deals with the first ideals of true life, and reveals to men the Divine purpose for them today. These are His first lessons."[89]

The following list of Christ's commands are produced here to help give disciples today some idea of what it would have looked like to follow Jesus in the first century and to pray for grace to do the same today.

No.	**Text**	**Command**
1.	5:12	Rejoice and be glad (when personally opposed)
2.	5:16	Let your light shine before others
3.	5:17	Do not even imagine that Jesus opposes the Law
4.	5:23-24	Leave (worship) go and be reconciled to offended brother
5.	5:25-26	Settle serious problems with others quickly
6.	5:29-30	Deal seriously with whatever leads you to sin
7.	5:34	Do NOT swear or depend on establishing your veracity byinvoking God in an oath
8.	5:37	Think carefully before speaking and always tell the simpletruth. Be true to your word
9.	5:38	Do NOT take the law into your own hands

10.	5:39-41	Endure loss for the Kingdom by allowing personal insult(turnthe other cheek for a slap), property loss (cloak), and forcedservice (going extra mile) rather than grasping on toworldly ways and personal rights and privileges.
11.	5:42	Give to the one asking and loan generously
12.	5:44	Love your enemies
13.	5:44	Pray for your opponents and persecutors
14.	5:48	Be perfected by love—by God filling you
15.	6:1	Do NOT serve to be seen by others
16.	6:2	Do NOT draw attention to yourself when giving to the needy
17.	6:3	Be secretive and behind-the-scenes in helping others in need
18.	6:5	Do NOT pray insincerely, to be seen or heard
19.	6:6	Pray in secret
20.	6:7	Do NOT pray using thoughtless, repetitive words

21.	6:9-13	Use "The Lord's Prayer" as a model for prayer
22.	6:16	Do NOT fast to impress others with your sacrifice
23.	6:17	Fast only in God's sight, not in others'
24.	6:19	Do NOT make any earthly thing your treasure
25.	6:20, 24	Set your heart on eternity and work for God
26.	6:25,31,34	Do NOT worry (about your physical life or future)
27.	6:33	Seek to advance God's Kingdom and glory FIRST –all the timeand in everything
28.	7:1	Do NOT judge other's motives or condemn them
29.	7:5	Deal with your own sin FIRST (repent in faith)
30.	7:6	Do be discerning and do NOT waste time on mockers
31.	7:7	Seek God's help through persistent prayer
32.	7:12	Always do to others exactly what you want done to you
33.	7:13,21	Enter God's Kingdom through the narrow gate of the Livingand written Word of God

34.	7:15	Beware and stay away from false teachers (whose lives betray their words)
35.	7:24-27	Hear and OBEY (practice) the words of Christ

Endnotes

[1] Juan Carlos Ortiz, *Disciple*, chap 11, pp 83-92; and later books: Cry of the Human Heart (chap 4- Children Quarrel, pp 29-39), Living with Jesus Today (chap 1 – The Eternal Babyhood of the Believer,pp 11-19) , and God is Closer than you Think (chap 16 – Having Spiritual Children, pp 135-143). This principle of spiritual immaturity and its crippling a believer is a cornerstone truth of what God taught Ortiz.

[2] See my, *Are You a Christian or a Disciple?* Part One chapters 1-4.

[3] The ministry that God has recently called me to is to hold **RBDs** (Renewals of Biblical Discipleship) globally and help Christians in Christian churches understand why they have stopped growing, digressed, turned their focus within the church's walls and become irrelevant to the lost of this world. Contact me at ed.gross@comcast.net for

information about coming to your city or church for a multi-church RBD.

[4] George Barna, *Growing True Disciples*, p 6
[5] Michael Wilkins, *Following the Master*, p 74
[6] Wilkins, p 132
[7] See the writings of Bill Hull, Jerry Trousdale, David Watson, David Platt and Kyle Idleman for great contemporary witnesses to biblical discipleship
[8] Wilkins, p 192
[9] Matt 10:38; 16:24; Mark 8:34; Luke 9:23; 14:27
[10] Matt 8:21-22; 10:21, 35-36; 12:46-50; Mark 10:28-30; Luke 11:27-28; 12:49-53; John 19:27-28
[11] Matt. 4:18-22; Mark 2:13-14; Luke 14:15-24 (18,19)
[12] Matt 13:44-45; Luke 14:33; Philippians 3:4-8
[13] See, *Are You a Christian or a Disciple?* chaps 6-8 where I discuss the subjects of Evangelism, Salvation, Grace, Faith & Repentance.
[14] Karl Barth, *The Call to Discipleship*, p 20
[15] From, "I Need Thee Every Hour" by Annie S Hawks, 1872
[16] Thomas a Kempis, *The Imitation of Christ*, p 104
[17] Deitrich Bonhoeffer, *The Cost of Discipleship*, p. 69
[18] Bonhoeffer, pp 45-47
[19] Ed Gross, *Let Love Win through YOU*, pp 23-24

[20] See my little book, Let Love Win through YOU (2011)
[21] Gary Badcock, *Nothing Greater Nothing Better*, p 30
[22] For an excellent book focusing on this truth read Paul Miller's *"Love Walked Among Us"*
[23] See Matt 26:25, 49; Mark 9:5; 10:51; 11:21; John 1:38, 49; 4:31; 6:25; 9:2; 11:8; 20:16
[24] From Jewish Encyclopedia.com, "Bet Hillel and Bet Shammai"
[25] Quote of Shammai in Pirkei Avot 1:15
[26] Eugene Peterson, *A Long Obedience in the Same Direction*, P 130
[27] From Judaism 101, Sages and Scholars, online.
[28] David Bivin, *New Light on the Difficult Words of Jesus*, p 23
[29] Jerry Trousdale, *Miraculous Movements*, p 85
[30] See Matthew 5:19; 15:3; 19:7; 22:36-38; Mark 10:3; 12:31; Luke 1:6; 18:20; 23:56; John 8:5; 12:50
[31] In NIV Study Bible, Leon Morris, Gospel of John editor, p 1656
[32] See John 13:1, 23; 14:21,23-24,28, 31; 15:9-10, 12-13, 17, 19;17:23-24, 26
[33] NT Wright, *Surprised by Hope,* p 288
[34] Acts 17:6-NKJV
[35] See the amazing accounts in **Miraculous Movements** and its sequel, **Father Glorified**

(Thomas Nelson Publishers) in which the authors show how non-believers all over the world have been led to Jesus by the powerful love of His children.

[36] Juan Carlos Ortiz, *Disciple!*, pp 12-17
[37] Wilkins, p 125.
[38] Kyle Idleman in *Not a Fan*, pp 32-33
[39] Bonhoeffer, pp 61-62
[40] Idleman, pp 130-32
[41] Gene Edwards, *Revolution: The Story of the Early Church*, p 104
[42] We used to sing the song, Take the Name of Jesus with you, in worship:

Take the Name of Jesus with you,
Child of sorrow and of woe,
It will joy and comfort give you;
Take it then, where'er you go.

Refrain

Precious Name, O how sweet!
Hope of earth and joy of Heav'n.
Precious Name, O how sweet!
Hope of earth and joy of Heav'n.

Take the Name of Jesus ever,
As a shield from every snare;

If temptations round you gather,
Breathe that holy Name in prayer.

[43] See Acts 1:16,24; 2:36, 39, 42-47; 7:59-60; 9:5 (22:8; 26:15); 9:34; 11:7-8; 12:17; 13:11; 13:47
[44] See Acts 14:23; 16:14; 18:9
[45] See Acts 20:19,24; 22:17-21; 23:11
[46] Gene Edwards, pp 107, 108
[47] Brother Lawrence (aka Nicholas Herman) in *The Practice of the Presence of God*, 1st letter
[48] Brother Lawrence, 2nd letter
[49] Brother Lawrence, 4th conversation
[50] See Matthew 1:22; 2:15,17,23; 3:15; 4:14; 5:17; 8:17; 12:17; 13:14, 35;21:4; 26:54, 56; 27:9
[51] NT Wright, *Surprised by Hope*, p 105
[52] Idleman, p 85
[53] David Bivin, *New Light…*, p 19
[54] See Matthew 18:15-20; cf. 2 Thessalonians 3:6-16; Romans 16:17-19; Acts 5:1-11; Galatians 2:11-16)
[55] Robert Banks, *Paul's Idea of Community*, p. 23
[56] Richard Longenecker, *Patterns of Discipleship in the New Testament*, p 59
[57] Karen Kogler, MA Thesis at Concordia University, the web.
[58] Come, Ye Sinners, Poor and Wretched by Joseph Hart, 1759
[59] Longenecker, , p ix.

[60] Longenecker, p ix.
[61] Larry Hurtado in *Patterns of Discipleship in the New Testament*, p 27
[62] Hurtado, p 26
[63] Hurtado, p 17
[64] Hurtado, pp 19-28
[65] Hurtado, pp 27-28
[66] As I have been challenged to repent and return to my first love, my mission has become "to follow Jesus and make disciples of love who will advance His Kingdom by multiplication and missional unity."
[67] See Acts 2:4,11,16-17; 4:4-12; 4:23-31; 6:3-10; 9:17-20; 10:44-48; 11:22-24; 13:1-5; 19:6 and compare them with the original promise of Acts 1:8 about what will happen when the Spirit empowers the disciples!
[68] If you need to sink more deeply into the love of Jesus and have Him help you see the other loves displaced by His love, you might be blessed by working through my short book, Let Love Win through YOU!
[69] CH Spurgeon in Eugene Peterson, *A Long Obedience in the Same Direction*, p 156
[70] Gene Edward, *Revolution: The Story of the Early Church 30-47AD*, 114-115.
[71] Bonhoeffer, *The Cost of Discipleship*, p 99
[72] Bonhoeffer, p 45

[73] Bonhoeffer, p 47
[74] Bonhoeffer, p 47
[75] Bonhoeffer, p 49
[76] Bonhoeffer, p 59
[77] Bonhoeffer, pp 63-64
[78] Bonhoeffer, p 69
[79] Bonhoeffer, p 75
[80] Bonhoeffer, p 97
[81] First generation = Jesus following the Father and doing His will explicitly, perfectly and consistently. Second generation = the apostles and other disciples who followed Jesus explicitly, imperfectly and inconsistently. Third generation = the disciples of the apostles, etc. who followed Jesus explicitly, imperfectly and inconsistently.
[82] Paul often found "people of peace" at whose homes he would stay, just as Jesus had commanded those whom he sent out in Mark 6, Matthew 10 and Luke 10.
[83] The word for "flogged" in this text refers to being beaten with rods not with whips. The Roman beatings were usually more civil than the Jewish floggings.
[84] My first discipleship-focused book, *Are You a Christian or a Disciple?* spends much more time making this point. Get it if you have any doubt that every Christian should be a disciple and every disciple should be a disciple maker.

[85] There are many good books and websites that have material devoted to the commands of Jesus. Just go to the internet and enter a search for "all the commands of Jesus" and ENJOY the fruit of many good brothers and sisters. Make sure you check out my "50 Commands of Jesus for Disciples Today in appendix 3 of *Are You a Christian or a Disciple?*

[86] See John 6:44-46; 14:26; 16:5-15; 1 John 2:20,27

[87] Tom Blackaby, *The Commands of Christ: What it Really Means to Follow Jesus*, pp 4-5

[88] Larry Hurtado in *Patterns of Discipleship in the New Testament*, p 41

[89] G Campbell Morgan in *Discipleship*, p 16

CPSIA information can be obtained at www.ICGtesting.com
Printed in the USA
BVOW11s2021160216

436957BV00004B/7/P